A GUIDE TO ENLIGHTENED PARENTING

A Psychiatrist's Spiritual and Practical Approach to Raising a Happy, Fulfilled Child

by Dr Tien-Sheng Hsu

THE EARLY SESSIONS

The Early Sessions consist of the first 510 sessions dictated by Seth through Jane Roberts. There are 9 books in *The Early Sessions*.

THE PERSONAL SESSIONS

The Personal Sessions, often referred to as "the deleted sessions,"are Seth sessions that Jane Roberts and Rob Butts considered to be of a highly personal nature and were therefore kept in separate notebooks from the main body of the Seth material. *The Personal Sessions* are published in 7 volumes.

"The great value I see now in the many deleted or private sessions is that they have the potential to help others, just as they helped Jane and me over the years. I feel that it's very important to have these sessions added to Jane's fine creative body of work for all to see."   *– Rob Butts*

THE SETH AUDIO COLLECTION

Rare recordings of Seth speaking through Jane Roberts are available on audiocassette and CD. For a complete description of the Seth Audio Collection, request our free catalogue. (Further information is supplied at the back of this book.)

For information on expected publication dates and how to order, write to New Awareness Network at the following address and request the latest catalogue. Also, please visit us on the internet at *www.sethcenter.com.*

NEW AWARENESS NETWORK
P.O. BOX 192
MANHASSET, NY 11030

www.sethcenter.com

A GUIDE TO ENLIGHTENED PARENTING

A Psychiatrist's Spiritual and
Practical Approach to Raising a Happy,
Fulfilled Child

by Dr Tien-Sheng Hsu

Published by New Awareness Network Inc.
Manhasset, New York

Published by New Awareness Network Inc.

New Awareness Network Inc.
390 Plandome Road (suite 202)
Manhasset, New York 11030
www.sethcenter.com
www.sethinstitute.org

Translated by Mei-Yung (Sumi), Tsai, Hannah Hung, Jennifer Soong, and Stuart Pollack
Cover Design: Michael Goode
Editorial: Nancy Ashley, Rick Stack

ISBN 978-0-9894058-8-1
Printed in U.S.A.

A GUIDE TO
ENLIGHTENED PARENTING
A Psychiatrist's Spiritual and Practical Approach
to Raising a Happy, Fulfilled Child

CONTENTS

ABOUT THE AUTHOR

DR. TIEN-SHENG HSU started his career as a family doctor at the Renai Branch of Taipei City Hospital and then decided to study psychiatry in order to gain a deeper understanding of how the human psyche affects the body. He became a psychiatrist at Taipei City Psychiatric Center and then served as the director of the mental health department at Taipei County Hospital. Apart from his background in orthodox medicine, Dr. Hsu has studied holistic health philosophies and consciousness studies for over 25 years. His combined knowledge and experience has resulted in his highly effective and unique programs for parenting, child psychology, and the treatment of physical and mental illness. Dr. Hsu is the author of 13 books and a frequent speaker throughout Taiwan, Hong Kong, mainland China, Malaysia, the U.S. and Canada.

INTRODUCTION
A GUIDE TO ENLIGHTENED PARENTING

This book is very special. It explores child rearing, education and family relationships from the perspective of body, mind, and spirit.

In my clinical experience, I see too many teachers and parents who do not have adequate answers to the questions, "how do we teach children?", and "how do we get along with children?"

I once heard someone describe education in the following fashion: Using current experiences and theories to teach children, and then expecting those children to adjust to the society of the future. Unfortunately, many current theories of how to raise children are obsolete at best. As I worked with parents and children over the years, I heard the worries of many educators, teachers and parents. I also saw the pained expressions on the faces of the parents of troubled children.

"Home," the place of humanity's most intimate emotions, is also at times the place of the most suffering. Children are the most cherished things in a parent's heart and yet parent and child are most easily hurt by each other.

Education is truly a joyful process of learning and exploration, including both the outward exploration of this world and the inward exploration of one's inner self, for understanding the meaning of existence. However, nowadays educational and familial relationships are covered with a thick layer of dust, too many goals, and too many demands, expectations and standards. This not only distorts the innate quality and the purpose of education but also hinders the natural flow of love and emotion in the family.

Some parents attempt to disregard the standards of society and what they perceive as the cruel demands of the real world; they wish only for their children to have a happy childhood and to take initiative in learning. However, when facing the institutionalized educational system and the society's demand for performance—and profit-oriented materialism—in their hearts those parents often painfully ask themselves: "If my desire and approach to providing my child a relaxed and happy childhood ends with the child being maladjusted, having trouble learning, and having regrets for the rest of his life, how can that be the right course?

Yes, we have many questions. Although there are many books about children's education and family relationships, they do not succeed in scratching the right itches. This has led to the amusing popular notion which states that "relying on the guidance of a book to rear children is no better than rearing them as pigs!"

I wrote this book, "Guide to Enlightened Parenting" based on the insights derived from the wisdom of the New Age master Seth, regarding the nature of children's psyches, and my own experience in clinical psychiatry. In my practice, I have treated many children who were suffering from problems such as emotional dysfunction, learning disabilities, poor concentration and maladjusted relationships. The purpose of this book is to help parents and teachers to thoroughly understand children's hearts from a holistic perspective. Further, it provides practical applications for addressing problems and raising a happy fulfilled child.

Many of the concepts in this book are not contained in contemporary education theory and may be unfamiliar to you. However, if you are a loving parent or teacher who desires to learn more about how to inspire the full development of a child's psychological potential, then please read this book with an open mind and heart. I believe the principles contained within will be of great benefit to both parent and child.

I hope that all parents, teachers, and children may happily and joyfully fly and glide in each other's hearts.

* * *

PART 1: HOW TO EDUCATE CHILDREN

Children are the mirrors in which we see our inner selves. We really cannot understand how to educate children from observing them from the outside. It is only after we discover the inner child that we can do so. Only after this inner child is seen, faced, accepted and embraced will we realize that the outer child does not need any teaching.

1. HUG CHILDREN MORE.

Most people have experienced being hugged a great deal when they were infants and toddlers, but when they became adolescents and then adults, getting hugged became much less common. This is because society believes any physical contact between people such as hugging or embracing has sexual connotations. As a result natural non-sexual contact between two persons has become taboo.

Anyone who has a household pet knows that animals like to be touched, stroked, and loved. When the master comes home, the pet rushes to him, clamoring for affection. It may even roll over and expose its belly for the master to give it a good satisfying massage.

And the same is true for children. Many research reports regarding infants indicate that the more physical contact they get from adults—the more hugs, the more kisses, the more strokes—the better they grow, the better they eat, and the better the emotional stability they have. They also have a lower-than-average rate of psychological dysfunctions such as anxiety, depression, and insomnia when they are older.

The New Age teacher Seth tells us that all physical bodies contain an integral "body consciousness" within each cell of the body which is in charge of their functioning as a corporal unit. This means that the consciousness of the human body is analogous to the consciousness of healthy animals, and that both animals and humans have the same eagerness to be caressed and embraced.

This eagerness for physical affection can easily be seen among animals in their natural environments. Many species clean and groom each other's bodies and hair, chase each other playfully, or lean up against each other intimately. And these activities continue their entire lives.

However, with humans, the situation is different. It was pointed out earlier that, in human life, one is probably embraced most often in infancy. After reaching adolescence and adulthood, any physical contact, including hugs, seems tainted by sexual connotations. What this means is that, in the natural state, the human body hungers for touching and hugs from family members, friends, or friendly strangers. However, adults are taught that even innocent physical contact may be looked upon as sexually suggestive, an act of foreplay, or a violation. Therefore, many natural forms of non-sexual physical contact between people have become taboo.

Must embraces be limited to lovers, or those of different sexes, and seem to be foreplay leading to a sexual act ? This is a distorted social phenomenon, especially if it applies to children growing up gradually. For, in their hearts they still crave caresses, strokes, or hugs from adults just as they got when they were very young.

Children long for hugs and gentle touches from the warm hands of adults, and to sit in their parents' laps. Nevertheless, adults, influenced by this distorted societal belief, may gradually build barriers in their hearts, become embarrassed, and distance themselves physically from their children. At the same time, they teach their children, "Never let strangers, including teachers, touch you."

Of course, this is supposed to be a protective measure to prevent children from sexual abuse. But has anyone noticed that when children are growing up, their body consciousness remains like that of a little dog or cat, longing for touch, strokes, or hugs while all those longings remain unfulfilled?

Because of this, two things can happen.

First, children will often become sick. Because of this sickness, children seem to have regressed to an infantile stage and thus are entirely cared for with gentle caresses, touches, and hugs. This kind of intimate physical touch is very helpful to bodily health; it alone will produce good healing effects, and it will also stimulate children's powers of self-healing.

Second, children will become less confident and lack a sense of security. They are no longer touched by a pair of warm hands, and no longer can take refuge in a loving mother's accepting bosom or in a father's strong and safe arms. Children feel alone and out in the cold. This creates in them a mentality of fear and insecurity.

Actually, many adults long for physical touch, the feeling of just a caress, a stroke from others; in their hearts, they know that this type of harmless physical touch is necessary for a person's physical and mental well-being.

However, because of contemporary culture's distortions, after entering adulthood all physical touches are seen through a thick layer of sexual suggestion. Therefore, physical touching with parents, siblings, or friends either of the same or opposite sex are viewed as taboo. They are allowed only between lovers and sweethearts.

What a horrible distortion! Humans don't think about sex all the time, and not all physical touches are related to sex or must lead to sex. Sometimes they are just simple expressions of friendliness between two persons. A simple hug is longed-for and needed by everyone.

Sometimes I think the main reason people go to body energy adjustment and massage therapists is to satisfy the natural human longing to be touched. This kind of touch awakens the inner child in adults—that child who is longing to be stroked, loved and embraced. When this loneliness is comforted, recovery from illness comes naturally.

Dear parents, it does not matter how old your children are. I strongly recommend that you get close to your children more often. Besides having heart-to-heart talks, give them hugs, gentle caresses and simple physical touches. These will add unexpected benefits to your relationship with the children and the health of children's bodies and minds.

2. EAT WHEN HUNGRY AND SLEEP WHEN TIRED.

Children are natural creatures who eat when they're hungry and sleep when they're tired. When they are new-born babies, they need to be fed every three to four hours, even during the night.

In general a baby's feedings should be spaced evenly throughout a twenty-four hour period.

As babies grow, the adults gradually increase the time between feedings until, eventually the baby's eating time is synchronized with that of the rest of the family and has three meals daily: breakfast, lunch, and supper. Snacking between meals is gradually corrected. Is this the right thing to do?

Children want to eat when hungry, and then when they have satisfied their hunger, even though their stomachs are only about forty to fifty percent full, they impatiently ask permission to go back out and play. However, in this modern society, their parents do not allow them to leave, and insist that the children eat until they are ninety to a hundred percent full. Moreover, the parents generally allow no snacks between meals to prevent spoiling the childrens' appetites. Is this kind of eating routine right?

What precisely is the right way for parents to deal with their children's eating habits? Will eating three meals a day enhance the children's health and physical development?

If you have children at home, you can see that children are natural creatures with unlimited energy, always crying, running, and playing energetically. Yet, when they are tired, they fall asleep easily on the sofa, in an adult's arms, in the back seat of the car, or even at the table. They are so trusting, peaceful, and sweet, that it makes the fact that a minute ago they were rascals very easy to forget!

Children have natural instincts and innate abilities. They know naturally that to sleep when tired and eat when hungry is the best regimen for healthy living. Children want food when they become hungry because they know that if they remain hungry for too long, the body will not receive the nutrients needed to keep their minds and bodies fully functioning.

They also do not want to eat too much; they know this will overload their stomachs and intestines and overburden the digestive process, thus decreasing the sensitivity of their consciousness and their ability to learn, as well as their mobility, and the ability to focus.

When adults gradually change their childrens' habit of eating when hungry and sleeping when tired, the connection between children and the energy of the universe weakens. They gradually move further from the source of their deep unconscious, their joyful laughter gradually decreases, and their ability to learn plummets.

The three meals a day routine is not right for children. It results in overeating during the day, and staying hungry too long at night. The density of sugar, protein, and fat in the circulatory system varies too much from day to night. This gradually causes chronic illnesses in adulthood, and plants the seeds of degeneration in middle- and old-age. Children are the kind of creature who falls asleep at any time and anywhere into a complete and relaxed sleep. It seems as if their souls have returned to the depths of the universe, of nature, and draw afresh on its energy until they are full. When they reawaken, they are able to run and play totally unbridled.

This pattern of sleeping when tired and awakening after a sound sleep is the waking and sleeping pattern of all animals in nature. Their periods of being awake and asleep are separate and distinct. When they are awake, they engage completely in the activity of the physical world, and when they are tired, they never hold on, and take a nap immediately, and are rejuvenated after the nap.

Many adults have lost the habit of sleeping when they are tired. They very often don't grasp when they should rest. As a result, their bodies and minds are over-tired, and they have lost their flexibility; thus, they find it difficult not only focusing while awake, but also relaxing completely while asleep. Such a person cannot feel the kind of vigor resulting from a good sleep.

When children grow and start school, the habit of sleeping when tired is gradually broken. They are unable to have a good nap when they should, and this leads to inadequate concentration, a short attention span, poor memory, easy annoyance, and decreased ability to learn. The most important point is that children gradually lose their amazing ability to utilize the tremendous energy of the universe, and the vitality of their bodies and minds starts to decline.

Dear parents, is your child hot-tempered, unable to focus while learning, irritable and cranky during classes, and does he or she get sick easily and often? It is better to try not to correct your child's habit of sleeping when tired and eating when hungry. On the contrary, you had better move your household routine and eating habits toward sleeping when tired and eating when hungry. No food or no rest throughout a long period will make anyone sluggish, and is a major cause of physical deterioration

3. IS IT RIGHT TO PUNISH CHILDREN?

While teaching children not to behave inappropriately, such as
by hitting others, grabbing toys from them, throwing and breaking things when they are unhappy, being rowdy in the classroom, not doing their homework, and being untidy, at the same
time should we not also help them to establish the line between
right and wrong, the suitable and unsuitable? By not teaching
them this, do we really mean to allow children to become indulgent and reckless without any restraint? Teaching them some
standards of discipline does not seem fitting to the human spirit. Exactly what should one do?

When talking about children's education, one topic which
needs discussion is "punishment." Also needing further exploration is the whole idea of social values regarding crime, repentance, punishment, or self-blame.

Social values, in general, dictate that when one commits
a crime, one must be punished. Thus, we have household discipline, school regulations, the laws of one's country, and inter-
national law. Everybody tends to use regulations and punishment to frame a person's behavior, or to define what consti-
tutes good behavior and what is bad. "Good" behavior is
encouraged and praised, whereas "bad" behavior deserves
scolding and punishment.

With respect to children's education, we still mostly follow
this line of thought. From the earliest stages, we start teaching
children by setting a fine example or by telling them what is right
and what is wrong in the adult world. For example, when a child
grabs another's toy, at the beginning an adult may respond with,
"don't do that." Some impatient adults may take the toy and

return it directly; other adults may use words, gestures, or a demanding tone to order the child to return the toy. Yet, some other adults could not care less; they do not see any big deal in it. They think, "If you are able, then come and get it."

This kind of interaction with children seems trivial, but the effects it has on the development of children's mentality and their future behavior are deep and long-lasting. Some parents will hit a child's palm gently or just flip the child over and spank his bottom as a punishment. Some will explain the whole issue of morality, define what is right and what is wrong, tell the child what he did wrong, demand that the child willingly nod and admit his wrongdoing, and then give him a light punishment afterward.

Still others do not care to use reasoning and start by spanking the child. Without regard to reasoning, at least a child dares not to do it again after a good spanking. Yet worse are parents who always nod their heads to show their approval no matter what their child is doing, rightly or wrongly; as a result, the child cultivates a mentality of, "I am always right and others are always wrong."

There is a very important point here. When informing children what behavior is appropriate and what is not, should the concepts of wrong-doing and punishment arise here? In the contemporary view of childhood education, the notion that "wrong-doings must be punished" not only is unnecessary but also may create very poor results.

When we are teaching children about inappropriate behavior (hitting, grabbing toys, being rowdy, etc.), they may not understand what is right or wrong, but shouldn't we at least set some rules or standards for them to follow?

The truth is that this way is not always right. After all, adults are the ones who set standards with respect to what is right or wrong. Some moral concepts and ideas of right or wrong are, to some extent, artificial. They do not really match the human psyche. Furthermore, after a child is punished for any wrong-doing, this child stops doing some things because of the fear of punishment, not because of a true understanding that doing those things is wrong or that the child's heart willingly restrains itself from doing those things.

Consequently, this may create two criteria of what is right and what is wrong. The reason they have not done certain things is their fear of being caught or punished; therefore, when they are sure that they will not be caught or noticed, they will continue those behaviors. Maybe they will be punished only one time out of ten; they will consider this worthwhile!

Another situation is that in which a child really establishes criteria of right and wrong in his heart and, because of the way he was treated by parents and other adults, he begins to form a strong belief that "wrong-doings must be punished." When this child reaches adulthood, he will use punishment to force others to say that they are wrong. This chastisement may be via legal enforcement or by physical force.

When this grown child knows he himself has done wrong, perhaps nothing illegal or maybe something for which he may escape legal punishment, his heart may still trigger a sense of guilt. Therefore, in his subconscious, he might decide that he be punished in order to compensate for the wrong-doing and to ease his guilt. The concept of "wrong-doing equals punishment" established in early childhood is gradually internalized to become a form of torment and guilt to plague his conscience as an adult.

At the subconscious level, many adults unknowingly attract "retribution" and "bad luck." They do not know that they make themselves suffer; worse, they make themselves sick. They endure torment from long-term illness so they can apply self-punishment, and self-redemption to make peace with themselves.

In my many years of research and exploration into body, mind, and spirit, I have seen that many things have happened to adults which may appear to be accidents, such as car accidents, other unlucky events, or physical illnesses, such as cancer, and that they are highly related to both this childhood view of punishing wrongdoing and an adult's "guilt mode."

After reading this far, one may be confused and think: "not teaching children any standards of behavior seems to be incorrect—I mean do you really want to allow children to become indulgent, reckless, and unscrupulous without restraint of any kind?"

On the other hand, teaching them is also scary because children might internalize the idea that "wrong-doings must be punished" and turn it into a moral concept in their minds. In the future, they might do something wrong that they could not help doing, or discover that they had unknowingly done something wrong; regardless of whether or not they were restrained by law, they could not overcome the barrier created by an uneasy conscience and it's need for self- punishment. What should one do then?

New Age spiritual education of children stresses:

1. Help children to establish their personal standards of right and wrong; besides the basic rule of "do not infringe upon others," everything else belongs to the rules of the game, and has no absolute right or wrong. Other than cultivating children's empathy, adults who teach children to understand others' situations and share their feelings with others also need to guide them to be responsible for themselves; children must learn to be responsible for their behavior, and not to depend only on the external rules to define what they can or cannot do.

2. Adults may introduce children to adult standards of right and wrong, and inform them that they are the "rules of the game" for everyone. Being unable to obey the teacher and being rowdy in the classroom does not mean that one is wrong; it only means that such disruptions make teaching and studying difficult for teachers and students, respectively, and they are not going to like one who is disruptive. Thus, the children may make their own choices.

3. If a child makes a mistake, adults should help that child realize that he or she should both not repeat the mistake again and compensate the victim, if any. There is no need to introduce the notion of punishment. Some children make more mistakes the more they are punished: the more they are punished, the more they deliberately misbehave.

Some children dare not make a wrong move because they

fear punishment. Once no one is watching them, however, they will do whatever they want, regardless of whether they were punished before, or punish themselves later in adulthood. Punishment is unnecessary because it neither prevents the wrong-doing nor helps the victim in any way. Sometimes it is only a meaningless act of "justice" and makes peace with one's own conscience, and that is all!

I hope that all parents, when teaching their children in the future, will refer to the ideas presented here

4. WHAT TO DO WHEN A CHILD GETS ANGRY FOR NO APPARENT REASON.

Many parents share a common nightmare: children throwing themselves to the ground and having a temper tantrum when their demands are not met. They do anything to embarrass their parents; whether a soft approach or a hard one is used, or the parents talk sweetly, all methods are futile. In the end, either nobody is happy and the child is pulled from the scene by grabbing his hand or ear, or the child is granted whatever he wants.

Most parents handle their child's temper tantrums instinctually, generally following three patterns.

The first type involves "losing all power and position." When parents of this type see their child having a temper tantrum, they lose all their previously agreed upon positions, principles, and rules. Even worse, they relent; they will do anything to make the situation quiet and calm, and thank heaven, as long as the child remains calm.

This type of parent, who gives in immediately to the child,

will often have strong conflicting emotional outbursts with the other parent, who refuses or scolds the child. Once the parent relents, he or she becomes a steady supporter of the child, and the child can seek help from that parent. In this way, the child always gets what he or she wants.

The relenting parent may admonish the other: "Why are you so mean to the child? Why do you not educate using a loving approach?" And gets the response: "You have no principles! Sooner or later, this child will be spoiled! How can I teach this child anything if you don't co-operate? I give up!"

Children are intelligent, and learn such emotional blackmail in early childhood. They get sweets just by being noisy, and merely by being rowdy they appear to be right and force others to relent. This lasts until they enter school and join mainstream society, then they find out that other people do not give in to their behavior! Finally, they have a taste of their own medicine.

The second type of parent is the "sentence and execute immediately" type. Parents of this type think that children should not become angry. When children anger, regardless of the reason, it is always wrong. Therefore, when their child becomes angry, then, instead of asking whether the child has any grievance or physical discomfort, the parents usually apply a strict attitude to suppress the child's emotional expression.

This child learns early that showing emotions is not good and that one should suppress and control one's emotions. Having emotions implies moodiness, and one should not be moody in any way. The psyches of these children contain too many suppressed emotions. The children may be fragile and become sick easily.

Those emotions are meant to express a child's unhappiness and to promote communication with the outside world, but the consequences of constant repression include an imbalance of body chemistry and can lead to immune system dysfunction. As a result, this child will become sick frequently. Besides, they may become emotionally dysfunctional, always repressing their inner feelings, unable to find a reasonable way to express them.

At the same time, this inner imbalance accumulates: there are periods when the child is quiet, with no apparent mood but, when the accumulation reaches a critical point, he or she will suddenly have an emotional outburst seemingly for no reason. When such children become adults, they may follow the same pattern by constantly transforming the repressed emotions into all manners of physical symptoms, or become persons troubled by their moods for days at a time.

The third type of parent is the "detached" type. They are incapable of handling and facing the child's mood. When the child throws a temper tantrum, these parents block their own feelings and temporarily become wooden in order to conceal their frustration and embarrassment. They pretend they haven't seen it and that nothing has happened. This would seem to be a correct and intelligent solution, but the long term result can be very sad indeed.

Having been treated this way as children, as adults these children can develop signs of a sense of a separation between body and feeling. On the one hand, they can feel their emotions; on the other hand, the emotions seem so strange, they do not know whose emotions they are or what to do with these emotions. Moreover, because these children lacked guidance and got no mirror pattern (of their parents' reaction to their moods), when strong emotions arose in their adulthood, this often leads to so-called behavioral disorders. Some of the behaviors exhibited were even opposed to their inner emotions, and this can take them many years to understand what their true inner feelings are.

Here I offer parents some simple concepts and methods.

First, when your child becomes moody, let him know that becoming emotional is okay. You must also accept this "moody" child. The purpose is to let the child know that emotions are his friend not his enemy, and to guide the child to accept "the moody self" or one's own emotions.

Second, do your best to show the child how to experience the power of emotions, how to utilize these emotions in order to have effective and peaceful communication with others, and teach them to refuse any violations and any unreasonable treatment. Teach them that, when it is right to say "no" then say it! Help them to maintain a reasonable amount of dignity and sense of righteousness, and to use their emotions to boost the power lying deep within the body and mind.

Furthermore, if parents know how to balance their own emotions quite well, they can not only accept their child's moods but also help their child discover the beliefs that bring about the emotions. They can go even further, helping their child to delve within to the roots of their emotions and to the spontaneous and impulsive self there, and, to connect with this inner and deeper "sacred higher self." If you can follow the principles mentioned above to educate your children, I believe that the members of your next generation will have emotionally balanced and healthy bodies, minds, and spirits.

5. DON'T FORCE ADULT REASONING ON CHILDREN.

Adults usually do not wholly respect and take time to understand what is happening inside a child's heart. They may be very strict in their teaching and guidance, and they may do a poor job explaining and reasoning; thus, they force-feed a child's conscious mind with an adult's worldview and value system, and concepts of right and wrong. They completely miss the target of first capturing a child's heart, and then gently helping the child to gradually unify his inner world with extrinsic values.

I enjoy my counseling work with children and adolescents; it gives me a wonderful feeling. It is completely different from adult psychotherapy, and gives me a deeper understanding of how children's minds work and how they change into adults' minds. Of course, the more I learn, the more I am touched and moved. According to my observations, children's minds have many unique qualities, one of which is that a child's conscious mind is very clear—so clear it is just like crystal. Many adults' so-called subconscious motivations are clearly visible in a child's conscious mind. It is different from an adult's mind; adults need years of psychoanalysis and psychotherapy just to get a glimpse into it.

Another quality is that the conscious minds of children are quite unified. Their conscious minds know that they are the masters. Not simply that they are not controlled by the subconscious and unconscious, but that that they are in complete control of the subconscious, are capable, and can absorb unlimited information from the unconscious. This, also, is very different from the adult mind, which is filled with such a myriad of conflicting beliefs that it becomes clouded and opaque; its ability to perform is less than a quarter of that of a child's conscious mind because most energy is wasted in conflict.

Also, children's minds are very honest. Their existence is built on the trust that they have for the outside world and universe. They have an innate understanding that life cannot exist without trust. Therefore, children do not lie by nature. They are very honest to themselves and the outside world, and they easily open their hearts completely and wear them on their sleeves. They speak directly of their ideas, emotions, inner motivations, and intentions. Since children usually have not internalized the rules of right and wrong or the morality of adults, they don't feel they have to conceal their inner worlds. Sometimes, adults find their innocence and naiveté difficult to take.

I am telling you, the best word that describes practicing psychotherapy with children and adolescents is: "refreshing." One can see a lively, conscious mind uncontaminated by complicated social values, and containing no artificially-added values; they are spontaneous. Such a mind is so clear that it surprises me, and I applaud repeatedly. Most assuredly, once I gain the young client's trust, and have empathy and resonance with his emotions, the effect of therapy is swift—so swift that it is virtually immediate.

The child's mind is like a wilderness, where animals have never previously encountered humans; they are unafraid, and they come close to you to lick your hand and stroll around with you. Whereas doing adult psychotherapy is like walking into a hunting area of the forest; birds fly and animals flee from you. The result is that half of the effort is to gain trust even when the client is willing. Because the conscious adult mind has allocated a great deal of suppressed emotions and conflicting beliefs to the subconscious mind, it can only be described as very muddy and filled with land mines.

Children's conscious minds begin clear as crystal, and they are able to reach their unconscious areas unhindered. As they grow up, they learn many erroneous and contradictory ideas which cloud the conscious mind. This unclear opaque area of the conscious mind gradually becomes the so-called subconscious mind. Here I want to emphasize that this subconscious is a part of the conscious mind, and that the conscious mind has the ability to become aware of, reach, and take command of it.

This is an innate ability of the conscious mind; with honesty and courage, children and adults alike can become aware of their subconscious. One does not need years of psychoanalysis and psychotherapy.

I would like to explain further why children's conscious minds gradually become cloudy and filled with conflicting beliefs.

The main cause of this is that adults like to use reasoning with children. This reasoning by adults cleaves children's conscious minds and creates conflicting, opposing energies in their subconscious. You must wonder why this is so. It is simply because children have their own reasons for their every behavior and emotion. Adults may not know this at all. And if adults did know that their children had their own reasons, they might think that those reasons must be immature and not reasonable at all, and thus not worth paying much attention to.

However, these reasons, which adults see as immature and not reasonable at all, are usually based on the children's heart-felt feelings. (In fact, everyone has his own reasons!) Adults usually do not respect children wholeheartedly and take time to understand what is going on inside a child's heart. They may be very strict in their teaching and guidance, and they may be soft in explaining and reasoning; thus they ultimately force-feed children with their own value systems and their ideas of what is right and what is wrong.

They completely miss the target of first capturing a child's heart and then gently helping a child to gradually unify the inner world of a child's conscious mind with an adult's worldview and external value system. Many parents build an external power or colonial government in their children's conscious minds.

What is worth watching are the "explosions" which turn teenage rebellion into a revolution, until a unified power is established from the child's intrinsic beliefs and the culture of the outer world. Hey! This is a difficult process! Because of this kind of educational process, adults build layer upon layer of barriers and defense mechanisms in their conscious minds. After a while, they do not even know themselves the source of many of their subconscious motivations and the roots of their emotions.

Therefore, for the sake of us hard-working psychotherapists, I ask all parents next time, before you reason with your children, do not think that they know nothing and they are just blank sheets of paper on which you can draw anything and make a mess. Please bring forth your empathy and be unbiased in understanding your children's feelings and the reasons for their actions. The key is to catch a child's heart, and to interact with it in order to generate resonance. This will lead to a better result than force-feeding your reasons into the children, with a guarantee of no ill effects for the rest of their lives.

6. FEAR OF BEING ABANDONED.

"I am afraid that he does not like me; that he does not want me anymore"—the fear of abandonment by loved ones is a nightmare deep within the hearts of many, including both children and adults. This kind of deep-seated insecurity affects the development of a child throughout its life and is seen in the form of low self-esteem, unassertiveness, frequent reliance upon others, and, of course, a diminished ability to learn.

A human being is not only an independent creature but also one who has the desire to be adored by a loved one, expects warm friendship from a companion, and hopes to be accepted, validated, welcomed, and liked. All of these reinforce a sense of security in our existence. They also weave the tapestry of human social interaction. Therefore, it is a good idea for parents to look into their children's sense of security, or lack thereof, beginning in early childhood.

Babies have a strong connection with parents, especially with their mothers, in their daily routine in the physical world and in their spiritual growth. This is a source of security in early childhood. Everybody knows that people open their hearts only when they feel safe. While babies crawl forward they often look back to ensure that the open strong arms are still there waiting for them. In this way, babies build their sense of security until they can feel free to pursue their curiosity by exploring the world.

Here, I wish to slowly awaken everyone's memory. When you were still a child, did you hear your parents say these words? Or as a parent, have you said these words to your child?

"Don't call me mother (or father). Because you don't listen

to me, you are not my child."

"If you don't listen any more, I will give you away to others."

"Don't come back home if you dare do anything else!"

"From now on we are no longer related: because you don't treat me as your parent, I shall likewise not see you as my child."

Of course, we all know that most parents either love their children dearly or they try very hard to love their children. However, people can become extremely angry and emotional, and use words which will long be remembered in the children's future. Worse still, some words are used in jokes, "You were adopted—you are not ours." Words like these can later make many children want to run away from home, looking for the nonexistent "real" parents.

Therefore, let us not forget how innocent and naïve children are, and that they readily take words seriously. This kind of fear and worry that their parents do not want them may terrorize them for the rest of their lives and become part of their personality, manifesting as insecurity, fear, anxiety, and easily becoming stressed.

Many adults' fears of running out of money, having no friends, and having no intimate companions come from early childhood experiences of insecurity and a fear of abandonment.

Other than that, children have many other reasons, real or imagined, to feel insecure. For example, "If I don't listen to my parents and don't try harder to achieve what they expect of me, they are not going to like me or love me." Let us open our hearts and ask ourselves where a child who feels unloved can go? He may even be stripped of his sense of a secure existence!

I would like everyone to go down their memory lanes and ask whether your child might in his heart worry that his parents do not love him, do not like him, and that they might give him away any time. If so, please bring that child forward now and gently tell that child "It is all right. First, your parents were not serious; secondly, I (the adult self) am here for you and it does not matter when or where whatever happens I will always love you, support you, be with you, and I will never abandon you."

If you are a parent now, it does not matter how old your children are; you must let your offspring know:

"My child, it does not matter what your performance is, whether you have listened to us, or whether you achieve what we expect of you. We will always love you, and we will never abandon you!"

"My child, it does not matter whether we are angry, heartbroken, or disappointed; you are always our child!"

"My child, we would rather see you happy than be a high achiever but unhappy all your life."

Remember: it is never too late to say those words to your child starting right now—speak of it from your heart!

7. MY CHILD, I WANT YOU TO BE BETTER THAN OTHERS.

"Have you no pride?" "Have you no shame?" "You have fallen far behind in your studies in school, and are still grinning impishly and fooling around. You are really mixed-up!" What parents fear most is that their children might not care whether they win or lose, succeed or fail in life—because this attitude may hamper their children's upward momentum and their ability to compete, and thus be excluded from the competitive game of life.

We are taught from an early age that ours is a competitive society; even if we're not prepared to give away all our possessions, we still compete mercilessly. We think that if we let our guard down for just a minute, someone might stab us in the back. We fear we might become out-of-date as time progresses. We engage in competition with small groups of individuals, with large societies, and countries.

One person competes against another, one family competes against another, one social group competes against another, one enterprise competes against another, and one nation competes against another. We believe our own value is enhanced from defeating others in all these competitions. Not only do we build our own lives' perspectives around these values and think this way, but the whole of society, the newspapers, and magazines all encourage readers to think this way.

To most adults, life is like rowing against the current: "if we do not move forward, we will fall behind." While we rest or play, others will quietly catch up." Children do not believe as deeply as adults that living is so difficult. Children are too naïve, play too much, are insufficiently aggressive, unfocused, and pay too little attention to succeeding. Therefore, the educational system and adults have invented the word "honor."

"Have you no pride?" "Have you no shame?" It seems that in the educational atmosphere and in every level of society, competition is promoted as an ideal: through competition there will be winners and losers, and having the desire and pride to win and not to lose, and having a sense of inferiority, pain, sadness, and shame after losing will generate the impetus to progress. If they do all this, then there will be a chance for success within an individual, a society, and a nation.

Most people have read, in Charles Darwin's Theory of Evolution, about the theory of natural selection, which seems cruel to them. Competition to survive is not just a game of Monopoly or a game of "winner-take-all." In nature, such competition follows the rule of "survival of the fittest." If you fail, this means your genes are inferior, non-competitive, and that you will certainly be eliminated mercilessly by nature or consumed by your peers.

When children are scolded, they may cry aloud, but soon they forget the incident and move on to play as if nothing happened. Many loving parents are happy to see their children being carefree, but at the same time they may worry a little: "if I don't treat my child a bit more sternly, teach him the cruel reality of competition, he might be bullied as soon as he enters school. If he does not do better than others in class, he might easily lose his confidence. Doesn't that mean that I have done him a wrong which will affect him for the rest of his life? Must I therefore continue to push the child hard to know shame and to work hard."

Allow me to make a few more points.

First, I would like to emphasize that Darwin's Theory of Evolution is completely mistaken, including the social Darwinism to which it led, with the weak being eaten by the strong, the fittest surviving, the unfit washed away. All kinds of competition occurs in society because of this mistake, so that, once a person stops trying to best others, this person will be overtaken by others in the same profession or by others in his generation. Following this theory has been a backward movement for human beings and their spirituality.

Some possible reasons for applying a theory like this to a child's education are that parents want their children to be better than others, or are obsessed with not allowing their children to fail from the very beginning. As a result, children are drawn into this painful process of learning. They do not know for whom they are learning, or what they are learning: "is it just for the purpose of winning?" Once this kind of life-perspective has become established, life becomes painful not only for the individual but also for society at large: the values are distorted. We feel as if others may take us for an enemy if we do not enter the competition—we may be attacked, hurt, or slandered. So we say, "Because I am already in the water, I might as well go with the flow." Honestly, humanity's adoption of the "survival of the fittest" theory is a real shame!

The greatest enlightened being, Seth, once mentioned that the nature of all beings is not to be competitive: for individuals, life should be a cooperative adventure with all other human beings and with all other life forms, all simultaneously seeking fulfillment.

Children innately have an impetus to seek the best way to express themselves in their lifetime—they want to express their creativity to their utmost ability. This is an impulse inherent in all living beings: to seek fulfillment. Children naturally compete with one another in their own games, in a desire to replace their old ways with new ones. By nature, they have honor and they know shame. However, many parents insist that their children try to defeat others.

Please answer this: would you ask a soaring eagle to run a foot race with a zebra, then subsequently scold the eagle for losing the game with "Have you no shame? Have you no honor?" People often ask me why their children lack confidence: it is because children have to look to others in order to learn whether what they have done is sufficient, or right or wrong: day and night they have been fed these kinds of ideas. They are criticized for lacking opinions of their own while growing up. They are told to always seek the opinions of specialists or authority figures. Is this right?

Consequently, I would like all of us to work together to change our culture, change the educational system, and lead all children to follow their own impulses regarding the fulfillment of their own values, to gain a real sense of self-acceptance and confidence, and not to have the delusion they must defeat others. Let us help the children to develop their own impulses of cooperative adventure with everyone and everything else, and to harmonize this world by adding their tender warm hearts to humanity.

8. TRUE SENSORY INTEGRATION.

Many parents demand that their children swiftly adjust their mindsets to living in their groups or communities, or that they orient their senses and focus on their actions precisely and effectively at the present space-time location—on "the now"—as swiftly as they are able in order to excel over their contemporaries in class and in life. The scary thing is that when parents suppress the unique character and imagination of a child, simply because they are in a hurry for the child to adjust effectively to this competitive society, the result may not be a successful future.

The fashionable phrase "sensory integration" means that during infancy and early childhood development, children learn to coordinate effectively and precisely all of the sensory systems including vision, hearing, touch, smell, taste, and sense of being, in addition to the mobility system of their muscular and skeletal development, including the coordination of large and small movements.

How children integrate their senses not only influences the way they learn, their ability to learn, and the speed at which they learn, but also influences their self-confidence in the future. For example, one child with a unique ability and excellent coordination of sound and movement went unnoticed, and he was never taught to utilize sound to enhance his memory and ability to learn. Instead, this child was seen as having problems with hand-eye coordination. He was criticized from an early age for being clumsy and awkward. As a result, a beautiful gem was broken and the shadow of inferiority set in at an early age.

A child's sensory and movement systems are far more complicated than we know. They are closely related to neural functions and the learning process. By definition, the brain is a psychological organization where events are created—this is its innate ability. Children spend more time than adults sleeping and dreaming. Their senses while dreaming are more intense than those of adults are. This is due to the need to develop the ability to coordinate and integrate the sensory system, language acquisition, and muscular movements. For example, in their dreams, children test the doability of various actions. They crawl, turn, and tumble in their dreams long before they actually do so in real life.

By utilizing this important inner motivation, the brain learns to manipulate and coordinate all the sensory systems and muscular functions. Additionally, some neural connections and patterns for mobility become established this way. Therefore, the possibility for children to grow in a predictable and beneficial way is established.

One concept which must be clearly understood is that the mind has an inner sense which operates outside of time and space, while the brain has the ability to create all kinds of events. As for children, they sense the plasticity of an event; something adults have forgotten about. The way the brain learns to form an event is the same way the muscular system learns to move in different directions. Yet the function of the brain comes from the inner mind: one can say that the brain is the biological copy of that mind.

What this means is that the mind senses an entire picture of an event which includes the past, present, future, and probable variations of the event, and also encompasses the psychological depth of each individual and group involved. For example, during the stage of a child's sensory development, when that child sees someone, he may see what will happen to that person tomorrow or hear what that person will say tomorrow, because his sensory functions are not fully focused upon the current space-time location.

A very important point is that the process of integrating and focusing the senses solely on time and space is, to some extent, a learned art because the safety and existence of children is very important to human beings. Children do learn eventually to control themselves in space and time, by gradually ignoring the pictures and sounds coming from past and future. But that natural ability continues to exist—children usually have in their subconscious a precognitive picture of what will happen in the near future. This may allow them to take advance action to avoid any life-threatening or otherwise dangerous situation.

Regarding the integration of the senses, over-emphasizing a focus on the present time and space in the material world, overly identifying with the material world, being tightly trapped inside the confines of time and space, and thinking that it is the only reality and that all information must come through physical senses will result in the loss of creativity, imagination, and flexibility.

However, the information which comes from outside this concentrated focus on the present is often from the wisdom and insight of the future which is often emitted by our greater minds, based on knowing the whole picture of an event or from precognition. This kind of information also helps us find a path for the future.

Gaining a true understanding of sensory integration will help our children understand that tomorrow will be a better day.

9. CONCERN FOR CHILDREN'S FUTURES.
Nowadays most parents send this kind of message: "Child, what about your future? If you do not work harder, then you cannot compete with others. How can we not worry?" Over-criticizing, being overly protective, and intervening too much: All of these forms of lacking trust may destroy a child's confidence and deplete his ability to face challenges. This not only destroys a

beautiful gem but also becomes a self-fulfilling prophecy.

All parents everywhere worry most about three things: safety, health, and the future.

Let us talk about the future! Parents worry that if a child does poorly in class then he will be unable to qualify for the most popular academic courses, and cannot attend even the least expensive public university. They worry that the child will have no future, no professional skills after graduation, or may work only as a manual laborer, and not in a white-collar profession, sitting in an air-conditioned high-rise. They worry that the child will not have a steady income, and will be unable to find a spouse or provide for his family. They worry that if the child's grades are too low, and his performance is unable to match those of his peers, they could not be proud of their child, and they could only shake their heads and sigh when colleagues ask about them.

My goodness! You poor parents! Wait until your child is one hundred years old: he will still be your child, and you will still feel the need to worry about him. (I believe this totally: when I reach the age of one hundred I will still have to behave as a child to entertain my parents.) Additionally, the future of the economy is in doubt, competition is worsening, and finding a job is increasingly difficult. Who knows what misery and horror society will meet in the future?

Once a month I go to Hong Kong to give a lecture. People come to find the solutions to the worries they have about financial crises and the future of their children. Once, all of a sudden, I had an epiphany: finances are not a problem, and parents never need to worry about the future of their children.

What do I mean here? I have spent nearly twenty years

thoroughly studying the material of the New Age sage Seth and gaining a deeper understanding of the spirituality inherent in children and in the entire universe.

When the universe gives birth to a new life, when spirit uses the elements of the earth to create a physical body, when a new member of the human race is about to be born on the physical plane, what changes in the social environment will be in store for this new life's physical reality?

Already the universal spirit (the "sacred inner self" or the "source self") of every individual has evaluated the situation beforehand, and knows in detail the challenges that this new life will encounter on earth. As a result, before each child is born, the pre-birth investigation of each earth-bound spirit and its life planning has been done. These spirits are also well equipped with the abilities they will need for overcoming the challenges they shall encounter in their lives.

What I mean to say is, any child who has been delivered or is about to be delivered (of course that includes old children such as you and me) carries all his or her potential and probable developments in that seemingly innocent and fragile mind. Those hidden abilities are not frivolous. They are calculated precisely to meet all possible challenges that each child may face in its life. They are tailored to meet individual needs to ensure that, no matter what or how severe the life challenges are, this child shall have useful abilities and endless spiritual support from the universal spiritual reserve.

To tell you the truth, the bliss which I experience as a human being is greater than the Christian Heaven, or the Western Pure Land (of Buddhism). In everyone's living reality, no matter how great the internal or external pressure or challenges which must be overcome, they are all blessed. Any necessary abilities are primed and ready to tackle any horror or merciless blow. We always have the inner strength to help us overcome our difficulties.

Throughout human history, this has been the reason that, no matter how impossible it may have seemed to surmount a difficult problem, our ancestors always showed great bravery and survived unimaginably bad conditions. They not only showed their great wisdom and endurance, but they also amazed us repeatedly with exactly how much potential human beings have.

Seth has repeatedly emphasized, "You have no limitations; you are unlimited." I would like to comfort all the worried parents in the world. You don't need to worry about your children's future because in their spirit they already carry all the potential abilities to meet the challenges in their future. You must believe and have confidence and unwavering trust in them.

To practice the aforementioned principles in life, you must observe your child closely, never intervene too soon, watch closely how he faces problems and what he does to resolve them in his own way, understand thoroughly how he meets external challenges, and how he adjusts and develops spiritual abilities at any time. Gradually gaining insight from those observations, you will send these strong messages to the child: "Child, you have an inner spirit that is connected to the mystical power of the universe. Child, you were born with the blessing and power of the universe. Child, no matter what happens in any given time and place, I trust you. Child, you have to trust yourself completely, and I love you."

Nowadays, however, most of the time parents send the following kinds of messages: "Child, money doesn't grow on trees. If you don't study harder then what kind of future will you have? Child, you don't have power; you cannot compete with others and you cannot deal with challenges. Child, you don't know how to do things and what you have done has never been good enough. How can we not worry?"

I wish that all parents would have some trust in validation, using guidance and encouragement to build confidence in their children, to develop their potential, and not be overly critical, or overly protective, or interfere too much. All of these ways of not trusting destroy your children's confidence and weaken their ability to deal with challenges. Not only is this the waste of precious gem, it is also the self-fulfillment of the worried predictions made by the parents—Oh my! This child is really just incapable and gives me a headache.

Oh my! Only a little help is needed to change your parental attitudes a bit. Try this because the situation cannot be worse than the way it is now!

10. TEACHING CHILDREN TO FOCUS.
When a child expresses a deep interest in a certain subject at school and devotes several hours to the subject each time he or she studies it, the child's parents start to worry. They are afraid that their child is interested only in one subject and is ignoring the others in the school's curriculum. The parents will then force the child to stop doing what he or she enjoys and instead ask the child to focus attention on other fields. By doing so, the child

starts to act as if he or she does not care, or gives insufficient attention to all the school's subjects. Blaming the child for not paying attention is what the parents will do, but whose fault is it?

Many parents and teachers worry about children's inattention or their inclination toward hyperactivity. Children with "Hyperactivity Disorder," by definition, meet three criteria: inattention, hyperactivity, and impetuosity. What worries people the most is that this disorder affects the children's ability to learn, their interpersonal relationships, and teacher-student relationships.

"Inattention" leads to rifts in learning, and answering known questions incorrectly due to carelessness. "Hyperactivity" affects order in the classroom—problematic children receive disdainful looks and extreme aversion from teachers, which then affects their self-esteem and leads to a lack of confidence and depression later in life. "Impetuosity" will hurt interpersonal relationships and easily leads to physical conflicts with classmates.

Therefore, determining how to cultivate each child to concentrate is a challenge in today's educational systems. A master of the modern age, Seth, has this comment: "In fact, children are born with a natural inclination toward concentrating." Children usually devote hours of focus into the fields and scholastic subjects in which they are interested. Unfortunately, children's habits of concentration are usually broken by parents or teachers.

This outcome often causes me to think deeply about the strategy of current educational systems for teaching children to focus. First, we must probe into the thinking behind today's educational system. The purpose of contemporary education is to help children to become socialized and to adapt to the mores and values of society. For example, we have included many subjects—music, arts, physical education, talent classes—in the curriculum. The children are expected at least to pass, or to achieve higher grades, in each subject.

Let us honestly examine our motivations. Is the purpose of designing these subjects and fields to inspire each child's true nature or to ignore their unique gifts and talents to force each child to meet social standards? Each child is special. By nature, children also know what is the best direction for opening their spiritual abilities from within.

Current educational and examination systems do not exist to reinforce children's natural ability to concentrate. Instead, a system of training is based only on standardized curricula and testing. Moreover, children are completely separated from their true nature because the adults are terrified that their children may lose their competitiveness.

In the end, children are unable to throw their hearts into the topics which previously interested them. They can neither ignite the fire of natural talent that resides inside them by using their spiritual focus, nor can they pursue their own chosen hobbies, and interests. Without these abilities, they are unable to build an unwavering self-confidence that may differentiate them from others. Is that not a tragedy?

I need only to ask you adults who are reading this to think about how far your own experiences may be removed from your deep spiritual focus. Do you know what your unique talents and interests are? Do you understand how fully you trust that you exist? Are you clear that your individual worth is unique? Do you know that you cannot be compared to any other human beings on earth? Are you familiar with your soul? Finally, are you happy?

True education should be customized to each child's centre of spirituality. Teaching materials and grading standards should vary accordingly. Children should all be valued for their individual dispositions, uniqueness, and interests. Respecting each child's unique spirituality will be the primary focus of any teaching, not asking them to achieve certain standards in every subject. Only a revised educational system oriented toward respecting children's dispositions is able to cultivate children with true integrity, into those who can exercise their talents fully and contribute to society.

Unfortunately, the current educational system does not respect each child's disposition but only demands conformity. If children are is unable to follow their dispositions from within and be inspired by them, they will never be able to know who they really are.. Modern education produces only children who participate in social competition, thus making the purpose of being alive be to compete for existence. Everything relies on adaptation as its basis of reality.

The result is that everyone turns away from their internal dispositions. The most terrible thing is that children are unhappy while the adults wail: "What is the purpose of my existence?"

Therefore, a revised, contemporary education should be based on the belief that children's internal dispositions should be respected. Encourage, guide, and inspire them according to their natural inclinations. Do not destroy this kind of concentration by forcing them to focus on fields that do not interest them (you must at least allow them to develop interest in new fields, must-n't you?), lest they become confused about their abilities, lose their perspectives, and be criticized for not concentrating!

11. WHY DO CHILDREN LIKE TO PLAY VIDEO GAMES?

Why do children like to play video games? Modern society is no fun for children. For adults, making a living is of the utmost importance whereas, for children, having fun is. They like to go wherever the fun is. It is not hard to imagine kids, one after another, relying on virtual worlds in video games when adapting to the real world becomes increasingly painful and difficult.

That children like to play video games is the biggest headache for parents today. "Playing video games and reading comic books are bad habits" has been the impression with which the parents of this generation were reared. They are terribly worried when they see their own children devote time to video games, ignoring homework, eating poorly, and pulling all-nighters to play online games.

A reminder up-front: when we probe into anything, we should focus not only on its negative aspects, but also on its benefits. There is a reason behind everything that exists in this universe. If the benefits of something are not understood but, instead, presumed to be bad, then modifying the situation successfully will be difficult. Thus, we must ask, what benefits does the playing of video games bring?

First, it helps children to build their interpersonal relationships. Playing video games has become a common subject of conversation among children. If a child is completely foreign to the games played by others, he cannot join in on any discussions. So, how can he develop good interactions with others? Besides, playing online games together fills the provides a needed group activity, just like when we played in the playground in our youth.

Second, it trains the coordination of children's hands, eyes, and brains. The patterns of video games nowadays are versatile and require swift reactions. A child must devote his full attention to gaming. He not only uses his brain, but sometimes he needs instant hand-eye co-ordination to play; otherwise, he will fail.

Third, while playing the game, children can fully enjoy leadership and autonomy. They can decide their own roles to play, choose their own weapons and marching directions. By doing that, they enjoy the success or failure that results from their own decisions, and not from listening to their parents.

Fourth, it is a way to give children a sense of achievement. Some children do not perform well in school and are sometimes criticized by parents and teachers until they feel ashamed. By hiding in the virtual world of video games, they can be the bosses and sweep away all the failure and sense of loss which they experience in the real world. The sense of failure when they are criticized by parents and teachers over their failing grades is replaced by cumulative successes from gaming. Why not?

Fifth, children can avoid an unharmonious atmosphere at home by playing video games. They can delve into video games in order to self-heal, especially when parents are fighting. Some children with busy parents may find refuge in playing video games and online games.

Sixth, there used to be broad fields, clear streams, numerous countryside games to play, and mountains and forests in which the children could gambol and caper. Children today mostly live in the pigeon cotes of the concrete jungle—immediately upon stepping out of their house, they are on the street. They have private tutors, after-school lessons, and extracurricular classes to attend after school and, if not those, the grandparents' house is the place to which they must go during holidays. Therefore, children delve into virtual spaces and games with great immediacy—otherwise, where can they go?

After seeing all these benefits, will you, the parents, put more thought into this? If your children live without video games, where else can they go? If children cannot build confidence in the real world, must they kill themselves? In the nuclear family nowadays—parents, and one to two children—if the family atmosphere is awful, won't the children suffer? Thank God there is a world of games in which to hide.

Moreover, modern society is no fun for children. For adults, making a living is of the utmost importance whereas, for children, having fun is. They like to go wherever the fun is. It is not hard to imagine children, one after another, relying on the virtual worlds in video games, when adapting to the real world becomes more and more painful and difficult.

Therefore, I have a few good solutions to help children spend less time playing video games.

One of them is to make life more joyful and playful, and not just running back and forth between buildings and having endless homework to do. Bring the children to nature, perceive the beauty in every creature and plant, and take adventure in the outdoors. In doing so, who will be playing video games out of boredom?

The second is to allow the children to participate in their family's responsibilities and decision-making. Children in the past learned skills from their parents, or even joined the production line, at a young age. That helped children to cultivate a sense of responsibility and feel their individual worth. In contemporary families, parents value their children highly, and thus put them under great pressure regarding their performance in school.

Unfortunately, only a small number of the children may be at the top of the class. Which means that the rest of the children are "over-protected" by their parents, so the only way for them to feel a sense of achievement is through the world of video games.

Therefore, parents nowadays should treat children as adults, respect their opinions, and allow the children to have more leadership and decision-making power. When they experience the joy of independence and the power of making decisions, they will not need to find their individual worth in the world of video games.

12. TEENAGE PETS.

Parents and teachers usually act as if they are reassuring "teenage pets:" "As long as you behave, and don't run around, you will mature in a few years." In fact, not only do teenagers want to study, they also don't want to be wheedled, protected, nor cared for like pets. They want confirmation of their talents, expect to exercise their abilities fully, want to contribute to both family and society, hope for a meaningful existence, to be valued highly, and to be productive. They also have many problems, for example: gang-fighting, racing cars, skipping classes, sex and pregnancy, drugs, and so on. These are the worst headaches for families and society.

If you want to say that teenagers are adults, then they are actually adults who are slightly ignorant, a little naïve, perform careless acts, and do not think before acting. However, if you think that they are simply children, keep in mind that they are probably taller than you are. Today's children mature swiftly and healthfully, and they speak clearly and logically just like little adults.

To be honest, teenagers are troublesome creatures. These creatures do not meet the standards of behavior demanded in adult society, but they also do not obey as little children do either. Teenagers seem like a group of monkeys in the forests: howling, jumping around, leaving behind the immaturity and incapability that accompany childhood, but they do not act as well-regulated (or spiritless) adults who follow a mundane path in society. They are like raging torrents, full of youthful vitality.

This is the most awkward period of one's young life. Teenagers' moods are like riding a rollercoaster: they do not even know who they are and what are they thinking. This is particularly true of students. Students have many more years of schooling than in the past—one may commonly see students who are approaching their thirties. The average age for marriage has also increased from the early twenties to the thirties or even the forties.

In other words, the period of adolescence was shorter for the teenagers in the past because they graduated from school, joined the work force, married, and had children much earlier; whereas nowadays teenagers commonly delay graduation or progress to graduate school, and worry less about forming a family. When a teenager looks to the future, the time for settling seems further and further away but, unfortunately, children nowadays tend to mature early. Thus, their adolescences are lengthened.

Teenagers possess a motivation to act which is lacking in children, but they lack the self-control and social experience possessed by adults. Teenagers are full of energy, but they are not usually able to be productive in the society. The societies of the past were simpler and their structures were more conservative. Those teenagers perhaps inherited the family's business or married and had children at a young age. Even though the freedom to choose one's own future was limited, they naturally became valued contributors to society and give themselves purpose.

On the other hand, today's teenagers are full of energy, but are expected only to "just study well." They are confused about their positions and roles in society and do not understand their purpose in, and value to, society. They really are like a group of wild monkeys, running around, getting lost on the path of life. Let us put some thought into this: how can a group of impatient monkeys not become a group of agitated destroyers of both society and family as a way to release their energy?

Our familial society seems to ignore the spirit, vitality, conflict, and struggle which exist in teenagers. Either we treat them as pets—entreat them, spoil them, comfort them—or we treat them as juvenile delinquents—frighten them, threaten them, and control them. However, to tell you the truth, these methods are outdated.

Any path to a solution must start from the teenager's points of view. Day and night, teenagers think: "Who am I?

What do I do with these infinitely energetic and uncontrollable thoughts? What is my purpose and what is the value of existence? What should I do to rise in importance and status in society? How should I perform so I can positively contribute to society? I want to be recognized!"

Therefore, do not treat teenagers as pets, please. An angry pet is quite frightening. Start to value teenagers, listen seriously to what they want to say, care for their feelings, trust their abilities, guide them to ensure the validity of their contributions to the society and family, give them something to do, treat them as adults in an internship, have them assume responsibilities and execute duties. Only then will they grow. Do not simply cajole them while criticizing their immaturity.

* * *

PART 2: THE DIFFICULTIES OF MATURING

Be honest and wholehearted parents and teachers!

Many people want to be good and responsible parents and teachers; but they forget, children often can learn the most from parents being truly themselves.

Be the most truly yourself, communicating with children with your true emotions, without posing or pretending.

Only in this way can we help children to overcome the difficulties of maturing.

13. EMOTIONS: LET ME ACT THEM OUT FOR YOU.

Children can feel any extreme anxiety or insecurity which exists in the family, but they are not able to use speech maturely to express or vent their negative emotions. However, they are natural performers. They can "act it out" for you. Often being sick is one example of this acting out.

Children are a part of their families' energy gestalts. The source of children's emotional obstacles, behavioral problems, and physical illnesses is not usually the children themselves. I sometimes even think that children's problems reflect those of their parents, those between the wives and mothers-in-law, and all their family's other problems.

Many parents cannot accept this statement. They prefer to think: "Of course they are the children's problems. The children have problems which cause me trouble and bring agony to our family! The problem which needs a solution is my child's, so why accuse me? Could it be my problem? Is it my fault? Am I the cause of the problem?"

From my point of view, I think—this escaping from self-awareness, the unreflective mindset, just hoping to solve the child's problem—is this "adult" way of thinking not the same way of thinking your children have?

Of course, I still empathize so I wear a smile on my face because I deeply feel this anxious couple is indeed facing some trouble. What often affects children most is the atmosphere of insecurity spreading throughout the family. This frigid environment, be it the arguing, the violence, the crying, the silent conflict, the shallow harmony, or the surging emotions deep inside, is the source of children's tremendous anxiety and insecurity. Children can feel it completely, but they are not able to use speech to express maturely or vent the negative emotions they experience.

However, do not forget that children are natural performers. When they cannot express feelings through words, they will "act it out" for you, as mentioned before. Frequent illnesses is one way they have of acting it out. Others are doing poorly in school, picking fights at school, stealing money, lying, wetting the bed, having nightmares, feeling insecure, bizarre behaviors, biting their nails until they bleed, or some kind of strange form of self-mutilation. This last one I keep seeing in the clinic.

Here is an example. A father brought his thirteen-year-old son to me for help. He described his son's weird behavior. Whenever a scab would form on his wounds, whether they be due to accidents or self-mutilation, his son would pick at the forming scab to allow the wound to bleed (he even squeezed the blood out) so that the process of forming the scab would continue. This led to the formation of many big and small developing scabs on his wounds.

When I studied this child's background and his interaction with his parents, I learned that his parents divorced when he was very young. His grandparents reared him until he reached junior high, then the father took him into his home. By then, the father had remarried and had two other children. The father felt an obligation to the boy, but they reunited during a rebellious period of the child's life. He worried that his son would make bad friends or behave poorly in public; therefore, his discipline leaned toward harshness, repeated criticism, restrictions, and lack of trust. Thus, a tremendous friction resulted from their interactions.

Let us first probe into the child's self-mutilation. The purpose of many children's self-mutilation or self-hurting is to deliver a message: "Nobody in this world pays attention to me. Nobody cares about me. No one will care whether I am hurt, bleeding, or even dead." The hearts of children like this, which used to be vibrant with life, become numb. "Because nobody cares about my feelings, why should I?" Therefore anti-social kinds of self-mutilation and self-damage continually recur.

I told this father, "You are the father of the child and you love him dearly, so you believe that if a parent only rears a child and does not teach him, then any problems are the parent's fault. However, remember that, in the past few years, even though your son logically knows that you are his father, he was not closely attached to you emotionally. He expected a father who could finally love him, understand him, and care about his feelings.

"You, on the other hand, exercised the authority of a

father—you wanted to correct him, to mold him, to change his habits and behavior. However, think about it: Who was the one who dumped his child at his grandparents' house? What the child needs right now is not your discipline. The more you discipline him, the less love he feels from you and so he becomes worse.

"At this time, you should first start showing unconditional love, acceptance, listening, and understanding. Wait until the child senses your love, feels secure, trusts you, and understands the flow of emotions between you and him. By then, you will not even need to instruct him—he will naturally improve."

"Educate with love" is not only "love and not educate," but "when love happens, interacts, and flows, education will then follow."

14. THE SENSITIVE CHILD'S HEART.

The way you view a child will be the way he looks at himself later in life. Sometime, you might have scolded a child who did poorly at school by saying, "Why are you so stupid?" in order to shame him and create in him an urge to achieve. This single statement would then have passed directly through the child's conscious mind into the unconscious mind.

Children's minds are very sensitive. Many words an adult may have said to a child, which the adult may not even remember, are imprinted in the child's memory. They profoundly affect his or her development, emotions, and actions later in life.

The development of personality and the "self-image" (how one looks at oneself and values self-worth) are neither fully developed nor stabilized during early childhood. Once their self-image is fully formed, children will build their personality based upon it and will also structure their lives accordingly. Commonly, the formation of one's self-image plays the most critical role in forming a personality.

So how do children's self-images form? Once we know the secret, we can help children to build healthy and decent self-images that will influence their entire lives. Here, I would like to discuss a very important personality-forming process called "internal transformation." The way parents or adults view their children will be completely felt by them and become the most important reference for knowing who they are and believing that they are a certain type of person.

More clearly, the way you view your children will be the way they look at themselves later in life. Children do not possess the defensive mechanisms which may be found in an adult's conscious mind. For example, if your boss told you that you are stupid, you would not accept it. You would pretend to agree in front of him but think in the back of your mind: "You are the one with problems!"

However, before a child's conscious mind matures, he will not know whether or not he is stupid and will not rebel. When you say he is stupid, he will take the words to heart because he thinks that his parents are wonderful people who provide him with food, clothing, shelter… they are just like almighty gods! God's words are always "correct," and when a god says he is stupid, clumsy, bad, or disobedient then that must be true! Moreover, children will imprint the comments word by word into their subconscious minds, and, thus, stupid children, bad children, and children lacking in self-confidence continually appear.

Please do not think that I am being an alarmist or exaggerating the facts. Many adults overlook the effects of their words and actions on children, as well as their status in children's minds. In a young child's mind, whatever adults say or do, whether laughing or angry, represent his world, his god. Before his ability to differentiate develops, he will truly believe that what adults say is always correct. It may take some children a lifetime—through painful experiences—to understand both emotionally and logically that their parents truly love them. However, not everything they have said and done is correct because parents are humans, too, and they make mistakes.

Here is an example: An anxious couple brought their eleven-year-old daughter to see me in my clinic, the reason being that the girl seemed a little strange. Something seemed to weigh on her mind so much that she kept delaying things she knew how to do, and even forced her younger sister to do the work. This perplexed the parents, so they came for help.

In the process of talking to the little girl, in the beginning, because she was unfamiliar with me and because of her caution, she did not talk to me but, instead, communicated only by nodding or shaking her head. I have my own methods of resolving this sort of situation. In this particular session, I deeply empathized with the girl and what was troubling her. Eventually, she started to tear up, and it seemed as if she shed all the pain of being misunderstood throughout all of those years. Tears flowed down her cheeks.

It seems that the little girl fell out of favor after her younger sister was born. The situation would not have been too bad if that were the only cause. Her mother repeatedly told her

"She is your little sister. You are the elder sister. You should love her and let her have the things she wants." Oh! This makes a child feel not only that the love from parents was stolen, but also that she is blamed for any arguments she has with the little sister. She is not a saint. She was already quite unhappy for not being understood and, yet, she was forced to accept that "you are the elder sister; you should give precedence to her out of courtesy." That is impossible!

Additionally, while the younger sister grew, the mother continued to tell the elder daughter, "You see, even your little sister is better than you!" After learning that, I totally understood why the little girl did not want to do any work and simply reassigned it to her sister. When I told the little girl "It is not because you do not want to do the given tasks; it is because you are afraid you cannot do a better job than your younger sister does, while being scolded. That is why you do not do them." The tears poured from the little girl's eyes, from having been mistreated and misunderstood, when she heard what I said.

Therefore, I strongly advise all you parents that how you view your child today will be how the child views himself tomorrow. All words and actions from adults influence their children greatly.

15. INSECURITY.

Many parents discover that their children are insecure: The children are anxious when the adults are absent; afraid of going to the washroom by themselves; afraid of the dark and unable to turn off the light to sleep; cannot concentrate on their homework when their parents are not around; cling to their parents and do not allow the parents to leave their presence ("separation anxiety"); are afraid of taking initiative to make new friends; are being bullied at school but are afraid to defend themselves, and are even afraid to tell their parents.

All of the above are phenomena representing children's internal insecurity. If this problem is neither faced nor handled, as the child matures, it may manifest as various physical and mental conditions: frequent headaches or stomach-aches; often having a fever and cold; recurrent asthma; the need to visit many hospitals and clinics; or eventually becoming neurotic. Examples of neuroses include anxiety disorder, panic disorder, obsessive-compulsive disorder, social phobia, anorexia, bulimia, and crazily shopping without satisfaction.

Therefore, insecurity in children not only seriously affects their development, learning abilities, and physical health but, more importantly, it affects their accomplishments later in life. Many children who perform poorly do so not because they are insufficiently intelligent or lack ability, but because of insecurity which leads to a lack of self-confidence, and which further affects performance in school and during their career, and their interpersonal relationships and marriages.

Not every broken marriage is a result of extramarital relations. Even if the cause is extramarital relations along with some incompatible beliefs, the root cause is most likely due to the insecurity among the couples! Thus, probing into the causes of children's insecurity or discussing how we can cultivate healthy, brave, and fully confident children through a certain "body, mind, and spirit" education is something I believe is very important.

First, we have to build an important concept. Sometimes the insecurity in children comes from their natural sensitivity and their introverted personalities, but we have to remember that insecurity may be inherited. Whether through genetics; nurturing; verbal and non-verbal communication; or the parents' own insecurities about their own future, money, and health; all of these will deeply affect their children.

The following picture will form: That of a meticulous care-giver who is concerned about every possible danger and need which the child may have, and who will strive to protect and care for the child in the hope of giving him or her the greatest sense of security. Each time the child falls, the adults hurry over and, before the child can stand by himself, he is in the care-giver's arms. Even after the child has felt bodily pain and learned to cope with a mild graze, and even before the child may be comforted by Mother Nature, the care-giver prematurely intervenes to bring comfort and support as an outsider.

It seems as if the care-giver is trying to prevent the child from being injured and is providing the best protection and security. However, the opposite may possibly be the truth. What the child actually receives is not a sense of security from the caring, but instead he picks up on the care-giver's deep internal anxiety and insecurity.

Thus, the child is deprived of the opportunity to handle the situation by himself, and experiencing the process of getting support and presence coming from the inner self and from the natural environment. This means that, whenever he is without the care-giver, he feels alone, frightened and insecure--all of which lead to a lack of self-love and continuously asking for love as an adult, while, internally, the feeling of emptiness and loneliness still exist.

When a child falls, if the surroundings are safe, supporting him with warmth and love, and being ready to give him help when needed, will be enough—do not run toward him and lift him immediately with nervousness and worry. A child will understand that the feeling of pain is an important natural phenomenon in life. Its presence neither is bad nor makes people feel afraid and weak.

Thus, a sense of security and power to face the danger will rise in his heart. A sense of being deeply supported and comforted by the universe will arise at the same time. In this moment, by himself, the parents' holding back will not make him feel weak and afraid, but, rather, the sense of security given by the parents, and the power and security which arise intrinsically, and the goodwill of the Universe, will be transformed into an internal steadiness and confidence within the child's psyche.

If the adults always intervene immediately and overly protect a child when he falls, is alone, or is mildly sick, then this child will be unable to develop the ability to protect and comfort himself. Moreover, a belief system and feeling of a deep intrinsic sense of insecurity ("I am weak and incapable to face outside danger," "the environment outdoors is dangerous," or "pain and loneliness are hard to endure") will be a vicious cycle. In summary, the sense of insecurity is reinforced.

Therefore, it is essential for modern parents to provide their children with a safe environment, and to be in control of a situation without intervening prematurely or being overly protective, thus allowing their children to build their own sense of security with their inner selves.

16. GROWING UP WITH A SENSE OF GUILT.

When a girl does not like to do "women's work," but admires her father's straightforwardness and sense of justice and, furthermore, is interested in the father's logical thinking and study, she may guiltily ask herself "Am I wrong?" She feels deeply frustrated and confused about the basis of human nature and the integrity of being, but has no idea why she is thinking that way.

On the other hand, when a little boy does not want to become a "manly" man—to fight, to compete, to study boxing—but his interests are more closely aligned with the mother's, be they sensitivity, carefulness, or sentimentality, he too may wonder: "Am I doing something wrong?" and feeling frustrated and helpless.

When children are growing up, their parents usually ask the little girls to look up to their mothers as role models, hoping they will develop the roles of being a woman, a wife, and a mother. Little girls usually like to stick with their moms, follow them in and out of the kitchens, wash vegetables, shop for groceries, fold the laundry, and make tea for their dads.

On the other hand, little boys are expected to grow into the roles of a man, a husband, and a father. They follow their dads fishing, watching and playing baseball, working part-time, lending tools to others, etc.

However, due to the intrinsic androgyny of each human being, sometimes a little girl does not resonate only with the mother's behavior, but she also admires her father for his braveness, determination, and strength. Maybe she will imitate her father's behavior, being forthright and carefree. Or, a little boy will love to help his mother with cooking or be drawn to her fashion magazines.

These unexpected behaviors in children lead to two consequences.

One is adult panic. Parents worry about children having problems with gender-identity. "Of course girls have to imitate their mothers. What is the purpose of imitating their father's behavior? To be a masculine woman? Are men not like men and are women not like women?"

Of course, many parents cannot accept this behavior, so the little girl is forced to conform to her mother's personality traits and social roles. Similarly, the little boy is forced to follow his father's and be a "virile man."

The other consequence is that the guilt inside children's hearts will be continuously incorporated into their ongoing process of growth. Whenever they feel a natural connection with the opposite-sex parent, they will immediately think it is wrong.

Having worked in the mental health department for clinical work and research for years, I am not surprised that the causes of depression for many people started during childhood, when the sense of guilt regarding gender identity was embedded. Moreover, the stronger the affinity with the opposite-sex parent children have, the deeper the pain and frustration, the more severe the distortion of personality, and, of course, the higher the level of pain in adulthood.

Every boy and girl wants to agree with, and learn from, both parents and expects to play the role of man or woman in a holistic way which embraces both masculine and feminine traits. They feel that the quality of their personhood is beyond the limiting frame of gender identity and dislike being squeezed into a single gender-mold.

However, society's family education makes a huge mistake right at the beginning. Boys are forced to conform to their father's behavior, and girls to their mother's. Children are innocent—they have no idea about the "mistakes" they make. And thus, the integrity of the psyche and the personality, and the cultivation of creativity, are seriously damaged.

A child's natural happiness, freedom, liveliness, and inner wisdom is defeated repeatedly in the process of maturing. However, that is just the beginning of the accumulation of guilt and the suffering of personality!

And when children start school, due to the fact that the educators are in agreement that boys must be lively, active, and strong in mathematics, and girls must be quiet, tender, and strong in history, the children's psyches become further distorted.

Please do not think that I am making a fuss or exaggerating. This is a fundamental and important key to solving the problem of children's sense of guilt while growing up.

For example, much discord between parents and children, including serious mother-daughter and father-son conflicts, facing each other like enemies, and the misguided belief that the discord comes from karma from a previous life, arises out of the silent resistance of children, upon whom a gender-identity framework has been imposed. Needless to say, rebellion, behavioral problems, and emotional disorders are all related to this issue.

Therefore, Seth says earnestly: "sometimes removing the societal beliefs about what behavior is appropriate for a father and what behavior is appropriate for a mother saves more children than it destroys." This statement calls for careful consideration.

17. CHILDREN WHO LOVE TO LIE.

Shelly is a fifth-grade student. She has a cute Japanese cartoon-character hairstyle and complex and quirky eyes. I believe that if this were not the last resort, her mother would not have brought her to my mental-health clinic. For some reason, Shelly's aunt and uncle reared Shelly after she was born. Her parents did not take her into their home until she was five years old. After Shelly returned to her parents' home, her mother started to feel that something was amiss. She discovered that Shelly had many bad habits. From her mother's description, Shelly was stubborn, shirked responsibilities, lied, stole, and took revenge upon those who had offended her.

Speaking of the ways in which Shelly took revenge, I do not know whether I should laugh or feel angry at her. Since Shelly's family is in the food-processing business, this little girl would sometimes sneak downstairs at midnight and secretly eat cookies and other processed foods. She even hid food in her room. Of course, when her mother discovered this, Shelly was beaten and the goods were removed. However, what happened next was even worse: Shelly took revenge. She made holes in the living room sofa with a box-cutter, and she threw her mother's favorite gloves and hats into the garbage (and covered them nicely). When her mother finally learned about this—ha ha!—the stuff was probably in the incinerator! Oh, and further, Shelly would hide the alarm clock and be proud of herself when her father was late for work.

All of the above are her special pranks. Her best trick is to tell falsehoods. Sometimes she would reveal that she stole, for example, buns from the cafeteria. However, she is so skillful that even the salesperson did not believe that she did it. Sometimes, when her parents discovered that a certain item was missing from the house or had been damaged, Shelly would appear to be wronged: "Why is it all my fault?" "Do you want to falsely incriminate me forever?" etc. Then she would yell and shout, cry aloud, and give a superb performance. After her parents came to believe that she neither stole nor vandalized, then would she say: "Aha, I've tricked you!"

I could see that these parents were about to blow a fuse. Children with problems like Shelly's are not uncommon. Many of these problems start when the children are reared by their grandparents or other relatives, perhaps due to the work, health, or financial problems of their parents after they were born. After the children are about four or five years old, or are about to enter elementary school, the parents then take the children back into their homes.

At this point, a big problem arises, which usually did not exist until after the children are returned to their parents. They are discovered to be "spoiled" and to have developed many bad habits. Therefore, the parents try their best to remediate the problem and start "corrective" education.

However, from the child's perspective, her aunt and uncle nurtured her from the day she was born. She was given everything she wanted. Additionally, they gave her a lot of caring, attention, and time. She was happy as a clam! What happened next?

Suddenly, a pair of "strangers" comes along claiming that they were her parents. How can a little child understand why they did this? She thinks: "This pair of strangers forced me into their home without asking me. Fine. But I don't know them. They have never taken care of me previously, so why do they think they can discipline me now? Not only can I not get what I want and the love I need, but now all I receive is scolding and punishment. I seriously don't know what I did wrong! Why am I suddenly falling from heaven to hell?"

When Shelly returned to her parents' home, she escaped on the third day. Come on, what does a little five-year-old girl seek outside her home? It is very simple: Shelly just wants to regain the feeling of complete love and acceptance and the feeling of getting everything she wants, and the feeling of being spoiled. What she thinks in her head is: "Who are these strangers? Why are they against me? Are these people so-called parents? I do not want these parents!"

In Shelly's mind, these strangers were not her parents, but the enemy. She felt as if she were a guerrilla trapped behind enemy lines—she had to survive. Therefore, the action of stealing may be interpreted as: "You are not giving me the things I request, so I have to take them myself. How dare you say it's stealing and spank me for that?" The action of lying means: "Is it wrong to protect myself from your scolding and punishment? If I don't lie, then how may I protect myself?" The action of hiding food is even more obvious: "I don't feel safe here. Storing materials for war is needed. Maybe one day I can support myself and escape from the control of the enemy."

Shelly's actions were normal and made complete sense to her psyche. However, her parents had no idea what was happening. They tried very hard to rectify Shelly's wrong behaviors in order to alleviate their own guilt stemming from lax discipline. But who knows? The more they rectified, the more rebellious the child became and, even worse, the child plotted revenge. The child would yell, "please do not force me!" Thus, the parents became upset with the child's suffering.

I want to advise all parents whose children were not reared by them that, when your children return to your care, take things slowly. Accept all of the behaviors formed in the past, regardless of whether they are good or bad. Show your love and unconditional acceptance. Wait until the day the children open their hearts and accept you as parents, then slowly guide them in the right directions. Never be impatient, otherwise good results will be difficult to obtain.

18. I JUST LIKE TO REBEL AGAINST ADULT WISHES.

Shelly, the child who knew how to extract revenge at a tender age, confused her mother for years: "How does a fifth-grade child have such a strong sense of self-awareness, a need to confront family members, and to be vengeful? Oh my goodness, is she really the devil incarnate?"

Moreover, the mother revealed, after each counseling session, that Shelly's actions were worse than before. She did not seem to realize that she was wrong, and she showed no sign of repentance. Her mother worried that her antagonistic attitude and rebellious actions would evolve into an antisocial personality, resulting in antisocial behavior and the committing of crimes.

Consequently, I asked her mother to leave the room for one consultation. After Shelly gave her consent, I finally had an opportunity to talk to her alone. Maybe it was because I had just gotten a haircut so I looked more like a brother than an adult, but she trusted me somewhat. (My dear reader, at this point you probably realize that I am a weird doctor with strange reasoning. However, after talking to me, many outcast children feel that they have found a confidant.)

Why does a child like to act against adults' wishes? Why does she insist on doing precisely the opposite of what she has been told? Moreover, the more one scolds her and punishes her, the more she rebels. Does this really demonstrate that human nature is evil? Moreover, when a child acts that way, does that mean she will become a problematic individual in society? Or is it karma, as from a Buddhist perspective, that this child is here to collect on karmic debt from her parents? Was she born to torture her parents?

Shelly is a great child. She told me that what she really wanted was to rebel against her mother. The more her mother demands that she stop certain behaviors or actions, the more Shelly insists on acting-out. I tried to go deeper into Shelly's inner world to see whether she really was born to be the kind of person who says: "Ha, my happiness is entirely built upon another's failure and suffering." Can it be true that the nature of her personality was so evil that she completely did not care about others' feelings, which led to dumping her mother's favorite jewelry and cutting the leather sofa with no regrets? Come on, she is a fifth-grade student. How can you expect her mother to re-teach her and to learn to love her?

I thought about the psyches of teenagers and adults as well. I do not know whether you have heard of, or had a similar experience to, this example: some people's mentalities are such that they rebel for the sake of rebelling. The more one person opposes a certain action, the more another insists on doing it. I remember a few marriage cases for which I counseled. The only reason for the husband or wife to marry was that his or her family opposed the marriage.

The strange thing is that, after many years of suffering and hard work and the family finally accepts the other half, that other half begins to believe that there is no need for this marriage, only then realizing that he or she never intended to marry the other person. The whole marriage happened simply because the family opposed it.

Shelly admitted that, the more the others seemed to hate her, the more bad actions she would perform to make the others hate her more. In a vicious cycle, her behavior continued to worsen and she started to understand which buttons to push to get others to hate her. Shelly's logic was: "the more you hate me, the more bad actions I will perform." Whether they tried to teach her patiently, to educate her with threats and promises, or punish her severely, they generated no positive results. Therefore, I asked her: "Do you like people hating you?" "Do you want your mother to hate you?" Shelly was sad and shook her head.

In a child's mind, it is natural that, if people love you, they will accept everything you do. "If they do not accept me or do not accommodate my requests, then that means they do not love me." This kind of reasoning occurs especially in children who were spoiled since childhood and got everything they wanted. Therefore, children of this type, who act naturally, believing that everyone should love them, agree with them, and accept them unconditionally, are terrified when certain behaviors or personalities cause adults to "hate them."

A child may be totally clueless about what is happening, so she becomes stubborn: "If you do not accept my behavior that means you do not love me and think I am bad," "I do not want to live in a world where nobody either loves me or accepts me." She insists on returning to the world where she was loved, supported, and given everything she wanted. She begins to rebel. She does everything to reject that world and act against her parents for not accepting her or not fulfilling her wishes, so that she can return to the world where he is loved and regain the love which used to be there.

Shelly told me clearly that she does not like that her relationship with her mother was worsening. She just wanted people to like her; however, when things did not turn out to be the way she wanted, she would involuntarily do things against others' wishes. She wanted to change, but no one gave her a hand. Therefore, I went deep into Shelly's psyche—her rebellious actions and vengeance were actually the wrong way to try to regain love. Shelly should be given the opportunity to realize that there are better ways to regain her parents' love.

Maybe her mother should send this kind of message: "Whether you are good or bad, you will always be my child. I will always love you and I will never give up on you."

19. SWALLOWING EMOTION.

Johnny had intermittent stomach aches and diarrhea which came and went. Sometimes he had to go to the washroom more than five or six times a day. The frequency of washroom breaks affected his academic performance. His parents took him to many hospitals and could not find the cause of the problem.

Johnny was a seventh-grade student, and his frequent stomach aches and diarrhea lasted for nearly a year, and had had many medical treatments, including a gastroscopy and a colonoscopy, but the cause was not found. Antacids seemed to help but, once Johnny stopped using them, the diarrhea resumed.

It was after approximately a year had passed without Johnny's condition having changed that his mother observed that, during a vacation, the frequency of Johnny's stomach-aches and diarrhea lessened a bit, so she began to wonder: does this mean that his symptoms are related to stress?

As a psychiatrist, I hope that all parents pay attention to their children's diseases, regardless of whether they are physical or psychological. Even if there is a confirmed physical diagnosis such as asthma or allergic rhinitis or an infection caused by a specific bacterium or virus, this could also involves "psychological" issues such as stress.

Johnny's brave mother, urged by her intuition and her love for her son him, finally took her son to the mental clinic for help without telling her husband.

(My dear readers, do not be surprised; many people need

a lot of courage to come to the mental clinic. Some even come behind the backs of other family members. They are just one step away from putting a mask on their faces. It angers me every time I think of it. Hey, I, Dr. Hsu, am not a monster, and am quite popular. Is coming to see me that scary?)

In the counseling room, a young face, which should have been full of happiness and liveliness, was covered instead with distress and seriousness. Johnny told me that his father cared very much about his academic performance. Ever since Johnny reached sixth grade, his father checked his progress in every subject. Johnny's academic performance and grades needed to meet his father's standards. Each time Johnny did poorly in any subject, even though his father did not spank him, he would scold Johnny for hours, especially after he had been drinking. "If you don't study hard, how will you ever amount to anything? You bring shame to the family."

Johnny, who previously had occasional nightmares, now had them nightly. They were all related to school, study, and academic performance, and became the source of Johnny's stress and anxiety. On top of that, he was an introvert who was not good at articulation, so he suppressed many of his feelings. Please do not forget, our digestive system is there to digest our food, absorb nutrients, and eliminate waste. It is not there to bear emotions, digest anxiety, or absorb nervousness. Therefore, Johnny's digestive problem was not due to any functional problem related to digesting food, but it was due to Johnny's trying to digest his many accumulated emotions, and thus eliminate them in the form of diarrhea.

After this magical consultation, Johnny's mother's concern

was strongly affirmed. Ultimately, we learned that Johnny's digestive system was fine, and that the diarrhea was caused by emotions and not by any corporal source. Johnny, like many children with similar problems, did not even need medication.

Even though his father was not present in the clinic, I still gave Johnny's mother three pieces of advice: first, I encouraged her to affirm Johnny's father's loving and caring toward Johnny. After all, not many fathers feel they can be that responsible these days. (Sigh, the best way to deal with men is to boost their pride. What can we do? Men are low in self-esteem and hold tightly to their egos!)

Next, I told her to tell her husband: "The doctor said that our child needs special care." (That was true. Johnny is naturally introverted and does not express himself well.) "The more you scold him, the more stress you put on him and the worse his diarrhea will become." Finally, do not forget to add this: "If the problem with Johnny's digestive system worsens, he will be unable to pay close attention in school and his grades will drop. That will shame the family more. What can we do?"

I also told her not to say to her husband directly: "The doctor said it's all your fault. It is all because you give our child too much stress that he has diarrhea. You need to change! I am a good doctor and I want to live for a long time. Please do not put me in danger. Allow the husband to think this problem through; do not humiliate him, and allow any changes he wants to make regarding his attitude toward Johnny's education come from his heart."

In the following sessions, I directed Johnny to express his anxiety and nervousness through words and facial or bodily expressions. As we know, food should go from top to bottom, not the other way around. Similarly, emotions travel upwards from the bottom. They must rise to the level of consciousness and, only then, may they be faced and treated. If emotions go from top to bottom, whether they are suppressed in the subconscious or are passed through the digestive system, they will eventually manifest themselves as neuroses, autonomic dysfunctions, or all sorts of disease and illness.

A miracle happened. After four or five visits, the diarrhea and stomach aches which had bothered Johnny for more than a year, were cured without medication.

20. VIOLENT CHILDREN.

Ming was a boy in the fifth-grade. He was brought to the mental clinic by his mother because he lost control of his emotions at home on several occasions, threatened his mother with harmful words, and even used physical violence. The mother cried from her heart: "He is my child, shouldn't he listen to me? Why can't I discipline him?"

When Ming was young, all of his behaviors and attitudes had to meet his mother's standards. If he did not obey his mother, corporal punishment would ensue. That means that the child could not have his own opinions because his mother's opinion was always correct and always the best. Even if he had his own opinions, they would be rejected.

Over time, while Ming continued to mature, he sometimes expressed his anger and discontent. "Why must I listen to you and follow your orders?" In dealing with the child's emotions, the mother's reaction was: "If he expresses these emotions at such a young age, what will happen when he becomes an adult?" Thus, she used her parental authority to reject and suppress the child's emotions, allowing no expression of any emotions.

This meant Ming faced an even bigger conflict. Not only did he have to meet his mother's expectations and standards without having his own opinions, but he also had to suppress his anger when his opinions were rejected. He felt trapped within a huge sense of helplessness. Actually, when Ming was angry, he felt powerful, and with that sense of power he could have argued and communicated with his mother. But when the "Ming with emotions" was suppressed by the outer environment and the teaching "I shall not have any negative emotions"—the 'angry self is wrong,' then, the anger had no place to exit.

Human beings cannot exist very long with the amount of helplessness Ming was faced with. If a person feels truly and completely helpless, then that person's desire to exist wanes. Therefore, at the psychological level, Ming needed to feel that he was powerful. Anger, at the very beginning, will not turn into violence if you let it follow its natural path. However, if anger is suppressed and turns into helplessness and hopelessness, it will finally be transformed into verbal and physical violence.

Why is dealing with violence so difficult, and why does violence occur repeatedly? It is because most people put an equal sign between "anger" and "violence," or believe they are an example of cause and effect. In fact, this concept is wrong. Repression of anger does not help to minimize violence but allows it to prosper. A genuine expression of anger will not be violent; only a person who releases anger in this way may develop tranquility in his mind. People may start to feel confused. "Is this true? Why is it different from what I have heard?" That is okay. Let me explain.

Anger allows people to feel powerful enough to vocalize their opinions and feelings, to communicate with others, to take action, and to fight for their rights. When the expression of anger is not allowed, or is believed to be wrong—"I should not have anger. Being angry is wrong, is bad," or it suppressed by the external environment—one's sense of power is lost. A sense of despair arises and the flame of anger will be vented as a twisted action or violence; for those who are filled with helplessness, that is the only way to allow themselves to feel powerful.

That explains why taking sudden violent action often happens to people who normally are perceived as gentle and polite. "Endure for a long time and there will be problems." The same concept applies to violent children. A violent event is always followed by a peaceful period of suppression: obedient, ingratiating, unemotional, and waiting for the helplessness to build silently. It acts as a pressure cooker; that an explosion happens is no surprise.

So, what should we do when facing violent children? First, parents must get rid of that controlling concept of "They are my children. They should listen to me." One's sense of power should be used to serve one's own life, not to force one's children to obey. Guide the children to an understanding and acceptance of intrinsic anger. Anger is not a bad or incorrect thing. It is your power. You can use it skillfully for communication and expression. The fundamental way to treat anger is by exploring its roots and redirecting it.

21. THE CAUSE OF AUTISM AND ITS TREATMENT.
The understanding of the causes of autism in today's child psychology is limited. We know only that it is related to an anomaly in brain development, but how does this kind of anomaly form? How do we prevent it? How do we provide effective treatment? We have no satisfying answers to these questions yet.

Clinical manifestations of autism include mental retardation, language-development disorders, and interpersonal communication barriers. The specificity of each clinical manifestation becomes clearer as the child grows. The severity and the clinical manifestation of each case are different. Some autistic children not only have mental retardation, but also cannot communicate with the outside world, lack eye contact with others, and can even have severely stubborn behavior. Some have normal intelligence, but the symptoms of autism cause learning difficulties, and barriers to interpersonal communication lead them to fall behind in their studies. Some autistic children have a high IQ but, because of the aforementioned barriers and difficulties in expression, their talents are usually buried or they are viewed as odd.

A book in the Seth series, "The Individual and the Nature of Mass Events," has a brilliant description of autistic children. Please do not treat autism as just a type of mental disorder in children; the truth is far from that. Autistic children belong not only to specific families; they belong to the entirety of humanity. They are the children of Mother Earth. Furthermore, autistic children represent the inner child in both you and me. The child inside each of us is more or less fearful. Therefore, as we try to understand the inner world of autistic children, we need to be aware and mindful of the inner children inside us as well.

In many cases, autistic children are the ones who have this kind of thinking: "This world is not a secure place." (Does this sound familiar? I believe many people have similar thoughts). "The best method is not to deal with the world."(Think about it, isn't there a part of us that does not want to deal with others?) "Thus, as long as one's needs and requests are met, that is enough."

Sometimes I feel that autism is not just a type of mental disorder in children, but it reflects the situation of the world today and a sense of insecurity everywhere. That is, we adults have formed a world which feels very unfriendly to the reincarnated souls, and there is a great chance to be denied, rejected, cheated and, even worse, hurt. Therefore, I would rather lock myself in my own personal world. Even if I become lonely, at least I will not be hurt.

The thinking patterns and behaviors of autistic children lack flexibility. They must follow their own protocols and cannot make mistakes. Additionally, autistic children are also afraid to make decisions. They would rather avoid making a decision than risk the chance of making a bad decision.

From Seth's theoretical point of view, this is not a one-way problem. Autistic children can sometimes be very intelligent mirrors, reflecting the unacknowledged fears inside their parents.

For example, I have many clinical cases of patients who have autism. After a series of sessions of intense counseling, one mother realized that, whenever she is anxious, her child's symptoms become more serious. I realized that this mother is avoiding making decisions regarding her marital problems and her extramarital affairs. One of the reasons she is afraid to make decisions regarding those issues is that she lacks independence. The other reason is that she does not know what to do if she makes a bad decision. The huge part of the mother which is fearful and afraid of making decisions is expressed fully by her autistic child.

In addition, autism symbolizes when a person believes that he is of no value, cannot trust the impulses coming from within, and makes decisions which (he believes) produce more harm than good. Children with these problems also believe that hiding their own abilities is much safer than utilizing them.

Please do not think this is only the characteristic of autistic children. Many adults believe this and act similarly; they lack self-confidence, fear making mistakes, prefer not make decisions but allow others to determine their fate, and sometimes fear expressing their given abilities because they believe expression means there are chances for failure and for attracting danger. Regarding this, Seth gave a thought-provoking quote: "life is an expression."

The key to treating autistic children is that when an autistic child is given full care with no worries regarding issues of survival, he will continue his autistic behavior. This is because the autistic behavior allows his needs to be satisfied without contacting the outside world. Since the child believes that dealing with the outside world is unsafe, we have to truly face and deal with our own fears and insecurities while simultaneously increasing the child's trust in the outside world.

I am not asking you to take "food" away from the child, but to build a safe and trusting connection between you and the child by allowing him to choose his own food and have him ask for food when he is hungry. This way, once the child steps out of his own world and connects with the outer world by receiving the "treat" on the table, he will gradually walk out of his inner world. It is easy. Because communicating with the outside world is not dangerous and one may get a tasty meal in return, then why not? So try it with your child.

22. IS MY CHILD "GIFTED?"

The definition of "gifted" given by psychologists is based on an IQ test score which is supposed to delineate a gifted child. This of course, is bound to cause sadness in those children who don't fall into that arbitrary category.

In fact, every child is gifted in his or her own special way.

To tell you the truth, modern day psychology relies totally on statistics and psychometry to process information about children, and its goal is to compare the "normality" of each child according to the "standardized" tests. The field of psychology has set "default values" to define many "normalized" measurements, for example, the IQ scale. Those ones who fall within the ninety-fifth percentile of the norm are viewed as normal persons; the ones who fall within the top 2.5% are considered gifted; the ones who fall within the lowest 2.5% are considered moronic. This group is further categorized as "borderline," "mild," "moderately," or "severely retarded."

Psychologists use a lot of rating scales. They include: an Anxiety Rating Scale, a Depression Rating Scale, a Young Mania Rating Scale, a Bayesian Test, a Sharrock Test, and so on. Take a minute to think about this: What is the fundamental basis which supports all of the hypotheses and philosophies behind all these rating scales and tests? They all have default norms and standards. When your thinking patterns, emotions, and actions fall within the norm, you are considered to be normal. If you fall outside of the norm then you are abnormal. "Abnormal" is usually used as a label to describe something which is not right, which means there is a problem, that something needs to be corrected, that someone might be sick, or that someone is a weirdo. No matter what, it is "abnormal."

This way of thinking implies that everyone is more or less expected to be a fully equipped, standard product. Psychologists have built a "standard screen" or "test" of human minds which may be stamped with a pass or a fail. The psychology which emphasizes standards creates anxiety in people, who begin to worry about whether or not they are normal, whether or not they are insane, and whether or not they are acceptable within the society.

Thus, people start to fear their own natures and uniqueness. What if their uniqueness and personal natures do not fit into the society's big picture, and what if they do not match a normal psychological standard? How may they see themselves as normal? On what may they depend to survive?

Dear readers, please think diligently about your life's journey from childhood to adulthood. Do you remember a certain moment or experience which made you realize that you have a superb ability in an area? At that moment of realization, you probably felt excited and a little surprised about your own distinguishing features and uniqueness. However, the excitement may then have been followed immediately by fear: fear of being different, fear of being the odd one in the crowd, fear of not being accepted by people around you, and even fear of being attacked and rejected. Thus, you may have started to ignore those abilities which you discovered and decided to get accustomed to being standardized and normalized.

How many gifted persons become mediocre because we ask for standardization and normalization? Throughout the past century, specialists in psychology, religion, and science have categorized the human mind as a by-product of materialism, as the essence of evil, and as a tool for survival, respectively. Nonetheless, everybody, individually and secretly, has experienced the power of that mind. We were once filled with the desire to accomplish things using our innate abilities. However, religion and science would tell you that it such leanings are either due to delusion, or a chemical imbalance in your brain; in other words: you are crazy. In the end you may conclude that it is best to be ordinary, to let yourself be mediocre. From then onward, your life might be boring and insipid, but at least you're normal.

Similarly, each child is a gifted child in his or her own special way. If you think that having a high IQ is the only was in which a child may be gifted, then you are completely wrong. The definition of "gifted" children given by the New Age master Seth includes many powerful abilities which many of us either do not understand or did not even know about.

For example, some children have the superb ability to

express vast depths of emotion. Children of this kind are able to understand deeply and express human emotions, and are even able to calm panicking adult souls. Another gift is "dream communication." The children's cerebral cortices are very active in the dream state and they can receive a lot of past, current, and future information in "dreamland." These children may skillfully utilize their creativity and the dreams in their daily lives, bringing the instincts, inspiration, and creativity captured from the dream world into the phenomenal world when they awaken. These insights had the potentiality to bring forth great inventions and innovations, thus altering civilizations. Unfortunately, many of these children are categorized by teachers as weird, mentally retarded, hyperactive, autistic or in some other way "abnormal."

Therefore, we need a completely new psychology and philosophy for our children's education. We should not normalize and standardize our children, thus causing the gifted ones to become mediocre, and the "retarded" ones sad. We should truly try to see each child's uniqueness. Each child is different; not one of them can be called "standard." Each child is able to express the wittiness, flexibility, curiosity, and learning-ability of human nature. No child is "abnormal." The only problem is that we do not know how to individualize. Because we have already been so misled by "standards," we fail to notice the gifts and abilities in each child.

23. "SCHOOL REFUSAL"

"School refusal" is the result of the advanced mental development or modern children. It means that children's minds have achieved a certain level of maturity which enables them to tell their parents straightforwardly "I don't want to go to school because I don't want to study. I cannot give a clear reason, but I know for sure that I don't want to go." Nowadays everybody knows that being a parent is difficult, and this example illustrates just how difficult it can be.

Xiao Xiang is a girl in eighth grade who recently came to my clinic, accompanied by her mother, seeking help. The main reason is that a teacher at school asked her to take a psychological and physical evaluations in order to learn the reason for her refusal to attend school.

One could say that "school refusal" is currently a fashionable term. It bothers me a little bit to know that "refusing school" could become a physical and mental syndrome. My dear readers, some of you may be close to my age, or perhaps a few years younger—let us keep that to ourselves.

During our school years, approximately from fourth through sixth grades, "school refusal" was unheard of. What we heard most of the time was that so-and-so skipped school and played outside, or some little kid did not want to go to school and ended up half-dead from being beaten so hard by his parents, who then brought him back to school by the ear. Either that, or another child activated the power of his subconscious mind and made himself really sick, thus not only avoiding the punishment but also having a legitimate reason for being absent from school.

To a certain extent children nowadays are blessed because they have the safety of being diagnosed as having "school refusal." These days parents are influenced by the idea of educating with love on one hand, while on the other hand are the laws regarding child welfare, which causes them to worry about getting arrested for child abuse. They do not really want to punish their children physically in order to make them go to school. My goodness, in our day, if we did not want to go to school, we had better watch out!

These are a blessing for the more extroverted, assertive, rebellious children, because they do not have to worry about being beaten or running away from home. Relatively timid children fear going to school because of the bullies there, or of not being able to catch up with schoolwork, and of being punished by the teacher. They dare neither to skip school nor run away from home. Truly, the best excuse to avoid school is to be ill, and this better be a real sickness, not simply fakery; it must be clinically diagnosed. The result may be more tragic if the absence is due to a faked sickness.

From another standpoint, "school refusal" can be seen as the result of the advanced mental development in modern children. It means that children have achieved a certain level of maturity which enables them to tell their parents straightforwardly: "I don't want to go to school because I don't want to study. I cannot give a clearer reason, but I know for sure that I don't want to go."

Therefore, parents have to face and deal with the reasons which make children want to avoid school. Society has evolved, hence the emergence of the term "school refusal." The relationships between parents and children do not have to be strained and in conflict. Children do not need to use sickness to protect themselves from going to school, and can instead give a legitimate reason to suit their purpose.

Speaking honestly, a school is an organization, an institution, and a competitive system. Is it suitable for every child? Learning in competitive situations is simply impossible for some children. Once they learn that they must compete or that others will compete with them, the fear of failure and the pressure from competition stresses them out. Concentrating on studying becomes too much for them.

Another kind of precocious child is exemplified by Xiao Xiang. Her parents divorced when she was about four or five years old. She matured swiftly in a single-parent environment. One of the reasons she did not want to go to school was because "other children in the class are childish." Even though she is in the eighth grade, from her physique, her manner, and the way in which she garbs herself, the nurse at my clinic felt that "she is more feminine than I am; her appearance is that of an adult." A quality peculiar to precocious children is not only physical maturity but, also in their thinking and their emotional and behavioral aspects, which are far more mature and rational than those of some adults.

This reminds me of what New Age master, Seth, once said: "From the perspective of historical evolution of reincarnation and the soul of the planet, the children born today are actually 'old guys.'" It means children of today are really our ancestors from generations ago. They already have had rich experiences from previous incarnations, hence it is possible that their minds are more mature and their abilities to adjust are better. Therefore, today's children demonstrate their unique selves very early, causing many educators to retreat in haste.

These precocious children are lonely and have trouble adjusting to the school's environment. First, they may not connect or make friends at all, and they have no desire to join what they see as an immature group. Second, in the classroom a teacher must consider the mental capacity of the majority, not only in the teaching materials but also in the attitude toward students. The teacher's attitude is that "it is all about the attitude of an adult toward children."

However, precocious children may have far richer life experiences than their teachers and they cannot find their places in any unified standardized educational institution. They have no problem with the schoolwork. They simply do not want to go to school. I have emphasized repeatedly: all children are unique beings, so they should get customized educations.

While this may not be possible in reality, at least everyone must know that standardized and unified institutional schools will be too simplified for some students. Those children who can adjust may have no problem, but, also the ones who are unable to adjust do not necessarily have a "problem" either.

I am not saying that we should destroy unified and standardized educational methods. I simply mean to say that, when inadequacies arise, we must find a flexible educational method and environment for those children who cannot adjust, and not stigmatize them as "problems," then give up on them.

24. MY SON IS GAY.

One of my patients, a ninth grader who was homosexual, told me, "I become emotionally numb when others call me a sissy." It was really heartbreaking to hear this. Some teenagers dare not tell their parents about their homosexuality because they think their parents are unable to accept it.

During my many years of clinical psychiatric experience, I found that most gay men are aware of their sexual orientation when they are in the first or second grade in elementary school or, at the latest, in fifth or and sixth grade. That is, they know their sexual orientation at quite an early stage. Children like that, in this stage, have few differences with others with respect to either their behaviors or their relationships. In the eyes of parents and teachers, these children are simply quiet, shy, and do not enjoy group activities or are less extroverted than other boys are, and they tend to be sensitive. Most adults believe that these are simply their children's distinctive dispositions.

However, this is a rather important stage—the primary juncture for socialization—in which the secondary sexual characteristics are not obvious yet, while the distinction between the two sexes gradually appears. This is when homosexual males build the psychosexual orientation of their basic character, which means that they are preadolescents who have had neither any boyfriends or girlfriends nor any sexual experience, but they know they are boys who like boys.

A homosexual is completely different from a pervert or one with a gender identity disorder. A homosexual male does not at all doubt his identification as a male. He may be more sensitive, full of emotions, and introverted, but mentally he knows that he is a male, a male who is not attracted to females but, rather, to males.

Whether this kind of sexual orientation is acquired due to the influence of the environment or to the intrinsic effect of genes has long lacked an explicit answer. However, in recent years, because genetic research has progressed rapidly and psychiatry has gained more knowledge of human psychosexuality, homosexuality is no longer listed as a category of disorder in the latest version of The Diagnostic and Statistical Manual of Mental Disorders in the U.S. That is, the phenomenon of homosexual behavior has gradually been accepted as one of the normal sexual orientations. Besides, according to much evidence, genes seem to carry most of the responsibility while the environment has little influence.

A homosexual male who becomes self-aware during his primary stage of development will go through a process of self-discovery which starts quietly and internally. He does not know what is happening, but he discovers what he is. This child starts to face the two most painful tortures of his life after he enters adolescence during the last few years of primary school and the beginning of junior high school.

On the one hand, hormones squirm impatiently inside the child's body, triggering the desire to have boyfriends. Due to the current developed state of the Internet, he may learn more about himself by entering websites oriented towards homosexuality. Additionally, if he has sexual urges, he may browse sexually explicit or pornographic gay websites.

There was an example in my clinic: a mother was unable to believe her eyes when she accidentally walked into her seventh-grade son's bedroom to see—two nude boys entwined on the bed. One was her son; the other was the ninth-grade boyfriend he met on a homosexual website. Examples like this keep arising one after another. The poor parents! These children and teenagers do not know how to protect themselves at all and they become sexually active due to a sudden impulse, which really worries people.

On the other hand, the choice to adapt to familial and scholastic environments has its own set of difficulties. Some teenagers dare not tell their parents about their homosexuality because they know that wouldn't be accepted. And if the parents do learn the truth, they may try to force the youngsters to "correct" their behaviors by threatening them: "Do you want us to kill ourselves in front of you, to make you stop being gay?"

The child might be baffled and respond, "It is not my 'choice' to be gay. It was you who gave birth to me, and then I discovered that I am gay. If you don't want me to be gay, then I can't be myself."

Although some parents fully understand this, they may choose to ignore it and withdraw, saying, "Dear, I can't help you. You have to be responsible for your own life." Children hearing this feel as if they are being abandoned.

And what about school? These children are often unable to identify with others; moreover, they might be teased, isolated, and insulted. And they won't know why: "Have I done anything wrong? Where is the fault?" During the process of learning, when most teenagers need identification and support from their peers, these children may be totally denied.

As a result, relationship obstacles and depression take form very early. Some even have thoughts of committing suicide. Exactly how horrible is the future awaiting these children and teenagers? Parents and teachers of the modern era, let us help them together!

* * *

PART 3: THE TRUE FACE OF LOVE

Love consists of three essentials:

Treating children with true respect and trying wholeheartedly to understand their thoughts without indoctrinating, spoiling, or scolding them.

Sharing true emotions with children; ensuring that they feel completely and wholeheartedly supported and accepted.

Observing carefully and understanding wholly the meaning behind children's every behavior without making decisions for them or overly interfering with or criticizing them.

25. SPIRITUAL PRENATAL EDUCATION.

Early Childhood Education (ECE) is a field considered important nowadays and its range even includes fetuses in mothers' wombs. In fact, much research has shown that fetuses have the ability to learn and react to stimuli. Women who have been pregnant have had the following amazing experience: The fetus seems to have physical reactions to the mother's emotional state.

Parents who are concerned about the next generation may start with prenatal education. For example, pregnant mothers should focus on the harmonizing of their own emotions. To settle their spirits they can listen to classical music or "prenatal educational music." Additionally, they can read books to inspire creativity in the fetus or read biographies of great people, hoping that the baby will become a great person in the future.

The expectant mother may take a walk outdoors accompanied gently by her husband, hoping the serenity and openness of nature can comfort the fetus. Some mothers even start to meditate and have heart-to-heart dialogues with their child in an atmosphere of spiritual tranquility.

Precisely how strong is the fetus's ability to feel? Besides being stimulated by sounds and lights from outside and reacting to their mother's emotions, what else can fetuses feel?

First, I would like to talk about a certain phenomenon. During the period immediately after a mother has become pregnant, due to metempsychosis, or the transmigration of the soul, most of the fetus-mother pairs have a predestined relationship, but the mother seldom notices this. In the early stage of pregnancy, a mother usually has a series of dreams which portrays the relationship between her and her fetus in a previous life.

Many mothers feel at ease after these dreams. Although they do not consciously remember them after they awaken, they already have made an agreement with the fetus subconsciously to resume their previous life cause. They will achieve the unfinished challenges in the previous shared life and learn from each other to develop the understanding and trust between them in this lifetime. Much of the discomfort in the early stages of pregnancy, such as nausea, vomiting, and loss of appetite, will thereby be reduced.

The relationship between mother and fetus is actually more fascinating and complicated than anyone has thought. What fetuses can feel is not merely external physical stimuli such as cold, heat, sounds, light, or atmospheric pressure. In fact, each cell of the fetus reacts to light, and fetuses "see" the world outside through their mother's cells. However, the images they receive are different from those of the naked eye. Each cell on our body has the sense of sight. The difference is that adults concentrate this function on the retinas but fetuses show this normal potential in all of their cells. This is the reason why some people with extraordinary powers can read using their fingers.

Fetuses not only feel every emotion of their mothers, but some also even know innately of their relationships with their mothers in a previous life and feel their mother's inner thoughts, perspectives, and attitudes towards life

The New Age master Seth stresses once again that children are not born as sponges or blank pages which teachers and parents seek to fill. On the contrary, their minds are already full of knowledge. Some parts of that knowledge rise to the surface for development and learning, while some parts are stored inside their minds as potentials for enlightenment.

At this point, the mother's thoughts and emotions play a crucial role, leading the fetus to develop its ability in some direction. If there is no definite instruction, these fetuses, so filled with potentialities and possibilities, will not be able to develop these to their fullest, and fail to focus in on the ideal personality and direction in life they are capable of.

The idea most people have that fetuses are passive learners is not true. Fetuses know ahead of time which family they will be born into, the condition of their health, and the socio-cultural environment in which they will be reared. Besides, they make mental preparations to absorb all of their mothers' experiences from inside the womb. From their father's genes they inherit the wisdom of life, some of which is related to the basic biological knowledge of the formation and cooperation of cells. Fetuses use this knowledge as a springboard for creating the potential for their own mental growth and the growth of their personalities.

Thus, the true idea of spiritual prenatal education is not simply listening to classical music, taking a walk, or regulating one's emotions. It is about the mother's understanding and the maturity of her own soul. It is an awareness of the wisdom achieved through the connection with and spiritual growth of the fetus.

26. AT THE BEGINNING OF LIFE.

Children are innately curious creatures. They often ask embarrassing questions which make adults uneasy. When I was a child, I said to my mother, "Mom, just tell me honestly. It's okay. I'm old enough to bear it. Am I really your child? If not, please tell me soon because I want to find my real parents." My mother did not know how to reply. Another common question is: "Mommy, where did I come from?" This kind of question is often classified by experts in Early Childhood Education as the beginning of children's interest in sexual knowledge.

In the past, parents usually used the following metaphor as an explanation: "Once upon a time, there was a very big bird. It carried you in a basket from very far away and delivered you to our home." How subtle!

Nowadays sex education like that seems old-fashioned. Parents now tell their children open-mindedly, "You are Daddy's and Mommy's sweetheart, our gift of love. You were conceived after we made love and were born after nine months' growth in Mommy's belly." Perhaps they will continue to teach them about the organs from which they were born. However, if children keep asking "What is making love?" maybe parents will still say, "You'll know when you are older."

But, honestly, where do children come from? What should contemporary parents tell their children? Certainly, modern medical science tells us that a child's DNA is composed of half of the DNA from the father's sperm and the other half from the mother's ovum. However, where does a child's "life," personality, and soul come from?

The ancient Chinese thought that children's lives were given to them by their parents; therefore, as the Chinese saying goes, "When the emperor wants the courtier to die, he dares not disobey; when the father wants his son to die, he dares not disobey either" and "Our bodies—down to every hair and bit of skin—are gifts from our parents, and we must not presume to injure or wound them." To disobey and rebel against parents is considered unfilial.

Thus, in ancient mythology, the third prince, Nazha, was not allowed to rebel against his own parents because of the above assumptions. He felt lost because he believed his body was given to him by his parents and that filial piety restricted him from rebelling. So Nazda had no choice but to commit suicide, return his body to his parents and adopt a lotus flower as his body. Only then did he gain true freedom and equality.

From the traditional Chinese point of view, parents and children are not naturally equal. But not every rebellious child would dare to follow Nazha's example by committing suicide— who knows for sure whether he may live again?

Much of a child's sense of guilt in early life derives from this point: My life is not my own, it was given to by my parents. If I do not behave myself and disobey their orders, will I be unfilial? Does life have legality? Will it be withdrawn by my parents?

These thoughts cause children to spend their whole lives "repaying" their parents for the gift of life, resulting in many inner conflicts between love and hate in children's hearts.

Speaking of the beginning of life, Seth has an excellent explanation in his book "The Nature of the Psyche:" children's lives are not given by their parents. Through their parents, their lives are granted by "All That Is" itself. The point is that the matter of life being given is completely without additional conditions. This means that children are not considered the parents' property but are respected as individuals with independent souls and development.

Parents must communicate this clearly to their children, "You don't owe us anything. Your life came directly from the universe, from nature and from 'All That Is.' We're happy to contribute to your growth and rearing you. We love you but you are always yourself. You don't owe us anything and you definitely shouldn't live for us. You have to live thoroughly to honor life, honor 'All That Is,' and honor yourself. "

Down deep children understand that their lives are not granted by parents and that they do not have to repay them heavily with their entire lives. They also know that their lives were not given by God with the conditions that they will be sent to Hell if they do not behave well. They also know that life is not formed accidentally by the random collision of substances.

All children know in their hearts that the earth is not their home. They know that they are from other places, and it's only because they truly love the earth and like to experience rebirth that they return to this wonderful place and have a relationship with their lovely parents.

Life is the greatest miracle in the universe. It arises from the most valuable and most sacred design. Therefore, it cannot be removed by anyone nor threatened by anyone or any power. Additionally, this gift of life enjoys the most complete follow up service—unconditional love, kindness, and support. This is most amazing, is it not?

27. TO EXPLORE THE INTIMATE BODY.

When children explore their bodies with an attitude of love and curiousness, they are often scolded or restrained by adults, and their little hands are moved away from their bodies. However, for children, exploring their bodies is a natural expression of loving themselves. They do not know what they have done wrong. Thus it becomes an early source of a child's sense of guilt.

Every child is born with an instinct for love and trust. Children's love is strong and enthusiastic, but they are wounded repeatedly.

As a psychiatrist with a holistic approach to psychotherapy, I am always surprised, or I should say, I sadly learn, that children's love and trust is the strongest, but not in a linguistic way. The relationships they build with others are usually the purest, the deepest, and most influential in their lifetime. Adolescents are a little doubtful and childish but, basically, their hearts are still clear and their feelings are sincere.

Adults, however, are completely different. They keep most of their feelings to themselves, not easily giving of their love and trust. Sometimes I really do not know whether this is a progression, or a distortion and regression of our spirits.

Children ride in this world through the power of love. They do everything with a whole heart and trust; therefore, they are able to investigate the world curiously and adventurously and face the future undaunted. The power of love is so great and strong that children love and identify with their parents fearlessly. They move their bodies and open their arms, hoping for heartfelt hugs and care.

Yet parents who are busy with their careers can only see that their children have three meals a day, and are unable to take any more time to keep one another company. Some parents do not get along well with each other and, when they quarrel, they may even involve their children in them.

Parents who are emotional, troubled, hot-tempered, and self-deprecating can ask of their children only that they behave well and make good grades. Some parents may not have been truly loved in their childhood and did not learn how to love others or how to express love. Facing their noisy children, all they can do is scold or ignore them, or choose to say or do nothing. Sometimes the parents themselves are just as immature physically and mentally as their children. They may even need to be comforted by their own children!

The German academic world has a famous saying: Children before three years old will not be spoiled by any amount of love and care. However, nowadays, most children cannot get enough love. Even their own expressions of love have been strangled.

Due to changes in society, the exploratory area for children's love is often limited to small families living in apartments. Some children do not have any siblings so they are able to love only their parents. When they exit the door, what they see are apartments, elevators, roads, and buildings. When they play in the community park, they see only strangers.

Where may children express their love? Because much of children's love has nowhere else to go, they start to give their fullest love to their toys, dolls, or imaginary playmates. If you observe closely, you will see that the manner, tone, and actions which children use to care for their toys is reflective of the great, intense, and strong love in children's hearts! They crave for their parents' love to be as whole-hearted as the way they take care of their toys, but instead what they often get are more toys, with the admonishment to "go and play with your toys."

Sometimes children really want to show their love to their parents. However, many parents are always busy, even at home, and push their children aside, or otherwise keep the children from bothering them.

Each of these acts creates a new open wound in children's young hearts, wounds which will gradually scar because of the frustration of love like this. Many people have done research of violent children and adolescents but how many of them have ever thought of why one lovable, naïve, and trustful child goes down a road of evil because of the harm caused by lack or withholding of love? This society has numerous indifferent adults. What would these researchers say?

In the early stage of childhood, children's expressions of love are often restricted. They cannot get enough expression and feedback from the real human world; their only recourse is to turn their love to the world of toys and dolls. Some even turn to the closed kingdom of their hearts, refuse to interact with the real world, and become autistic.

Children's natures are full of curiosity and exploration. Their lives are games and their games are their lives. They are full of love and they have great interest in sex. When they are restrained from this, they do not know what they have done wrong. Children simply want to express their love to themselves or show their love to their body because the essence of love involves exploration and understanding.

Children have always thought of their bodies as symbols of themselves. Thus, when the body becomes the forbidden zone for early self-exploration, children become unfamiliar with themselves and their bodies. In other words, they feel that loving themselves is somehow wrong. This is an early source of a child's sense of guilt.

As far as I know, some people are able to explore a lover's body with love but they are completely unfamiliar with their own bodies. Let us think about this seriously: Maybe you are selfish, but do you have the ability to love yourself? Are you capable of showing love to yourself and your body freely? Or do you have "yourself" and your body but are unfamiliar with them? Can you truly love yourself and your body? If not, you still have time to explore yourself and your intimate body with love and curiosity starting from today!

28. HOW DO PERSONALITIES ORIGINATE?

Is my personality formed by inherited genes, my parents, the environments of childhood, and society? If so, I can choose neither my parents nor the environment as the source of my personality. What if I do not like my personality at all? What should I do? Go with the current? Wait until my next life? Go to a psychiatrist? Attend a number of courses to learn how to grow?

Traditional psychology thinks that personalities are influenced by three major factors: The first is genes (half comes from the father's side and half from the mother's, of course); secondly, the familial environment in childhood (this includes the personalities of parents, the interaction between them, the similarities and dissimilarities of their teaching attitudes, the ranking of all siblings and their relationships); and the third is the social and cultural environment in which we gradually become assimilated (kindergarten, primary school, teachers, relationships with classmates of the same generation, etc.).

These three factors include intrinsic causes (or the natural temperament) and extrinsic formations, transmitting the message that on the one hand, we must pay attention to genetics; on the other hand, parents have to provide a fine childhood education and rearing environment, and the whole country, society, and the greater environment must match that, too.

However, despite concepts like these and their attendant actions, we still know little about the origin of children's personalities and how the external environment forms them. Therefore, even though we are already adults, when we trace back to our familial environments, rearing, and the process of the formation of our personalities, we are often confused.

Take myself as an example: I am always wondering which part of my personality comes from my father, which part comes from my mother (perhaps this can be traced back several generations into the past), which part comes from imitations of brothers and sisters, which part is due to the environment from my childhood, the treatment of my parents, or one sentence spoken by my kindergarten teacher.

Furthermore, which part is from my own unique nature? (From where does this part come exactly: genes or soul characteristics?) This leads to my profession. In my clinic, I often must help people explore how their childhoods have influenced their future personalities and help them build good personalities. Thus, this kind of question frequently lingers in my mind.

Everyone must have wondered spiritually where his or her personality in this life came from. I do not believe that you lack curiosity about yourself at all. Is reality like what traditional psychology says: that personality is formed by genes, parents, childhood environment, and society? Would that not be miserable? You can choose neither your parents nor the environment in which you are reared.

What if you do not like your personality at all? You will deal with it and go on with your current life. Maybe you will wait until your next life to be born into a good family, but who knows whether a 'next life' exists? You will visit some psychiatrist, participate in many courses for developing oneself, try very hard to remember back to your childhood (including the process of birth) and discover one after another traumas of your youth. Oh my goodness! This is so time-consuming! Moreover, it is expensive. You will spend much time handling this problem and crying. After a while, you will even go home and become angry at your parents: See what you have done!

Honestly, I myself discovered this matter quite early. I started to dislike my personality when I was in the fifth or sixth grade.

I was thinking, "Ah! There is no hope. My parents have already spoiled my personality before I became conscious, in my infancy and childhood." By the time I realized that, it was too late. I could only comfort myself with tears and make promises that I will not spoil my next generation. However, I was still not reconciled to it. Finally, in junior high school, I vowed to "rebuild" a personality I liked, and, in tears, I asked for my best friend's help. (Please do not laugh at me. All of which I said is true.)

However, I succeeded! I received a comment from my ninth grade homeroom teacher regarding my excellence in character and academic performance. I was moved to tears. Afterwards, (I think I do not have to mention that) I had another thorough realization after I encountered Seth's philosophy.

From a spiritual perspective, children choose the parents who will bear them while they are between incarnations (of course the inner psyches of parents will choose their children too). Children chose their familial environments before they were born and they arranged their own childhood environments in tandem with their parents. They did this to create or build their personalities and to accomplish the special challenges of this life.

This idea has two aspects. First, children form the personalities they want to have in this life by choosing their parents' genes, their personalities, and how their parents treat them. The other aspect is that the children themselves are souls which evolve continuously and they construct the personality flaws which they want to overcome and which arise via their parents and childhood experiences.

This holistic viewpoint is very inspiring. It completely destroys the narrow theories such as "external shaping theory of the personality" or "childhood decides one's personality, and adults choose to go to psychiatrists and overcome their childhood trauma." It not only helps us to discuss the formation of an acquired personality, but also helps us to become deeply in contact with the inner spirit who could then guide us in creating a personality we desire, and thus change the outcome of our lives.

29. SUPER IMAGINATION.

People can naturally understand the hearts and feelings of those around them through imagination and performance because we are born with telepathy and the ability to enter the hearts of others. This is so natural to children that they often speak directly and correctly, in ways that embarrass adults.

Children's imaginations allow easy use of their emotions and telepathies. When adults give advice, they often say "If I were you...." This kind of sensible communication usually has a different meaning for children. Children are curious creatures: they want to understand everyone including themselves. They are also innate actors who like to act not only as themselves but also as everyone around them. More importantly, they do everything as if they are playing games.

When children imagine they are others, they imitate their tones, actions, and habits. This is actually a "drama of visualization," and it has two functions: First, children can store in their personalities every character they have met in real life, books, or their imaginations. Deep in their consciousness, they compare their personalities to their most recent lives or next incarnations and practice them one by one in games, creating a personality which they think is the best and may be acceptable in the real world.

Second, children can initiate their inner talents for empathy and telepathy by pretending to be other people. They are so confident in themselves that they do not worry about losing their identity or individuality. They somehow manage to become part of the person they imitate through acting. They can feel that person's every emotion and life experience. To children, this is an impromptu performance, part of a life game. And this will not make them forget who they are.

Adults often have doubts: such as "I don't know what my son (daughter) is thinking. Why does he/she say words that hurt people and do things without any planning?" "I can't understand why my husband is so stubborn!" "Why does my wife always want to go out? Isn't our family good enough? Aren't our children cute? " or "I can't figure out my boss's mind and what kind of person he is. What should I do?"

The answers to these questions are very simple to children—just pretend to be the person whom you want to understand! You have to give impromptu performances based on your daily observations and rich imagination, and treat it as a game. While you are playing this "game," perhaps you can invite people interested in this to play your role so that you can see yourself from another perspective, or you can play several parts and pause at any time, stop abruptly, and resume.

Do you think that children are unable to understand how their parents toil? Do your children complain so much that you do not understand them at all? Actually, the family is the best playground. Perhaps you can try this: When you awaken tomorrow, exchange your role with your children--the reasons for this include not only to relax yourself or to teach your children a lesson but also to truly see through children's eyes, how, you, their parents, and their world, looks.

When you do so, you will learn that the children enter role-playing far more easily than you thought. They will definitely have more fun than you will and they will show you—maybe you are parents who are strict, boring, and disappointing! When you infuse your teaching with fun, you will find it more useful than becoming angry at children and nagging them.

As mentioned before, it is natural to understand the hearts and feelings of people because we were all born with telepathy and empathy. And it is natural, too, to speak directly and honestly. But only the children do this, and it often embarrasses adults when they do. So, as children mature, they gradually learn that most adults do not say what they actually think and they lie when they know the truth. Therefore, the clearness in children's hearts becomes increasingly clouded. After all, they are just children! Why do they have to face the rules of the adult world? Maybe I am being too serious. What I mean is that children start to be dishonest with themselves and they learn the rules of engaging the adult world, the so-called EQ.

Interestingly, children often play scaring games, sometimes scaring themselves too. The kind of screaming sounds they utter often make adults uncomfortable. However, children do so for many reasons. In fact, scary games have a dramatic tension which maximizes mental and physical alertness. The accumulation of hormones that is overly suppressed due to nerves is released. This method of releasing tension is a process of self-healing. Many chronic illnesses in adults result from too much accumulated pressure created by tension and the attendant accumulation of hormones.

Thus, I want to give you one of the most precious pieces of advice. When your children or grandchildren are playing, do not stop them any more; instead, you should put your identity aside and join them. After a while you will feel less trapped in your own narrow life. Your inner spirit will be happier and younger. Additionally, your body will miraculously become more and more healthy.

30. FAIRY TALES.

Although the world of fairy tales may be at odds with reality, children are still fascinated with its charm. However, if one observes carefully, one discovers that adults' lives are also filled with fairy tales. What manner of contradiction and conflict are we facing? Are fairy tales merely collections of daydreams which go against the ways of the adult world?

Let us start with something simple: "Fairy tales," as the term implies, are stories which are told especially to children and they are stories written for them to read. When some parents read fairy tales to their children, they are unable to help thinking that stories about Aladdin's lamp, fairy godmothers, magicians, and Santa Claus, are completely inconsistent with reality. Why do we still read these impractical and illusory stories? Are they helpful to children's academic performance, relationships, and adaptability in the future? If not, then why not allow children to face the real world at an earlier age?

The miraculous and magical colors in fairy tales, in addition to the sudden realization of great expectations, have gradually faded from the inner worlds of adults and reality. Children's fancies, the journeys of heroes, and the fulfillment of big dreams have already been shattered by harsh realities; people have already learned to accept their fate and no longer have any hopes. Sleeping Beauty met her Prince Charming, who came to her rescue despite all the challenges. Then he gave her a deep kiss filled with love to arouse her from her sleep, and then they lived "happily ever after."

Gender equality should also be considered in fairy tales, so sometimes unlucky princes are cursed and transformed into ugly frogs. At that time, beautiful girls will be tested. If what they see is not merely the frog's appearance, but also the courage and kindness in the frog's heart, then the disgusting kisses they dare to give with their eyes closed may immediately turn their lives from rags to riches

The story of Cinderella is even more interesting. What should we expect of an ugly duckling who is abused by her stepmother and bullied by her two sisters? What is left of her? Nothing! However, Cinderella kept her daydream-like illusions. Moreover, these illusions were perpetuated by the fairy godmother! Therefore, from the mundane to the miraculous, from pumpkin to wagon, from ugly duckling to swan, all which seems impractical becomes "dreams come true." The memory of the handsome prince, the beautiful palace, the glamorous ball—and then the glass slipper left behind, in the end becomes the only magical connection between the far-away dream and her real life.

Now you tell me, can these stories be read to our children?

The naïve princess thought the one who would save her was a handsome and brave prince, but he turned out to be a heartless man who took advantage of her, deceived her, and took all her money. Ultimately, he even fell in love with another woman. "They lived happily ever after" and became a poor couple who could not pay their loans and who quarreled every day.

Your dream of Cinderella has been realized but, in reality, your business has failed, debt collectors have come for you, and your house has been repossessed. Where is your fairy godmother? Who will come to your rescue? All of your confidence and expectations are gone, are they not? They only made people see clearly the cruelty of life.

Although the world of fairy tales is at odds with reality and only the children can be fascinated by them, nevertheless, if you observe carefully, you will see that life is full of adult "fairy tales," too. For example, Superman, who came to the earth from outer space, and is busy saving both the world and his cute colleague; bitten by a spider, Spiderman is able to leap and vault on the roofs and from wall to wall; an ordinary maid has a happy ending through the magic of the media; the world of Harry Potter, an adventurous magic world, is a globally successful phenomenon. Would these stories not qualify as fairy tales?

What kind of contradiction and conflict are we facing? Are fairy tales merely collections of daydreams that violate the way the adult world works? Or do they provide some kind of psychic illusion for comfort after adults encounter frustration in real life? Or are they reflections of the fantasies of children who have yet immature minds? Do they provide a start of growth when children no longer believe in fairy tales?

Seth, the New Age master, has mentioned that fairy tales are always the great messengers of underground knowledge. Fairy tales themselves are definitely not "unrealistic illusions" and they will not be at odds with the cruel and realistic world of adults. We simply forget how to interpret the meaning behind fairy tales, and we do not understand how to make use of the profound wisdom of Seth—"you create your own reality"—to apply the spirit in fairy tales to creation in real life. As a result, a wide gap appears between the two.

That is, fairy tales are too unrealistic, whereas reality is always cruel.

I like what Seth has repeatedly emphasized: Even the grass is full of great hope. Great hopes, born in all children, are built on one's confidence in the truth, in nature, and in the life one is given. Fairy tales are metamorphic myths. They form children's intrinsic religion. Fairy godmothers, Aladdin's lamp, magicians, and Santa Claus are other faces of the Buddha in the East and God in the West; and prayers in the temples and churches,are also what Seth called the inner God and the Buddha in us, the symbol of a sacred inner self. In the best fairy tales, the greatest hope is always the winner. Misfortunes, pressures, hungers, and frustrations may always be changed suddenly.

Fairy tales are not inherently faulty; magical power has always existed. However, adults are blocked by scientific and sensible thinking. They are too involved in "reality" to look at the miraculous sides of their souls. They think only about how to deal with their lives but they forget the magic wand in their hands.

Truly great motive power lies in the imagination to think

about the unrealized things. The magic wand symbolizes that imagination with the help of great hopes can make a wide range of dreams come true. "You are never given a dream without also being given the power to realize it. You may have to work for it, however." Not only do children need fairy tales, but also all adults could recover their confidence and great hopes—with the wishing-well in their hearts and the magic wand in their hands.

31. HAVING THE CHARACTERISTICS OF BOTH SEXES.

Many educational experts and liberal parents nowadays pay attention to the sex education of children. However, few pay attention to "gender education." What is "gender education?" It means that when you know your child's sex, you start to educate your child consciously or unconsciously according to your personal view of the gender roles, or you follow the gender prescriptions of your society and culture. I think that gender education must be looked at very seriously. However, most people do not yet understand its influence on people.

Let me give you an example: during the recent recession, some women visited my psychosomatic clinic because their husbands had been jobless for several years, which was stressful on the women because in addition to doing their usual household work, they were also working outside the home. Thus they were experiencing anxiety, upset moods, insomnia, and lethargy.

Naturally, I asked them about their husbands, and the response they gave me was interesting: "He's still looking for a job. He's kind of upset by rushing around everyday. Sometimes he just does nothing but read newspapers, watch television, chat with his friends, drink tea, or drink alcohol." When I asked, "Why not ask your husband to help you with shopping, taking care of the kids and preparing meals?" They all gave the same answer: "That's a woman's job! How can men do that? Even if they were capable of doing it, they wouldn't help!"

Some jobs considered traditionally to be women's work, are rearing children—playing with them, helping them with their homework—and preparing three meals a day, going to the supermarket, doing the housework, serving the older members of the family, etc. Men neither know how to do these jobs, nor do they think they could do them better. Some even say: "This is none of my business." Why do they say this? Is it possible that since we were young, our families, schools, and society have been doing much too well at teaching us that the genders have different jobs?

Many men are unemployed now. Losing self-respect at the beginning, some feel ashamed and are idle all day long, and some become alcoholic to escape from daily reality. However, I am thinking that there is one main reason why so many men are losing jobs now: they think they can only do "men's jobs."

Starting with family education, we strictly use the children's gender differences in choosing what they should be taught. For instance, boys should not cry. They should be independent and brave. If your boy is interested in Barbie dolls, designing clothing and cooking, or is sensitive and considerate, you may be afraid that he is a sissy or gay.

Girls, on the other hand, are not allowed to fight. They should be gentle, thoughtful, and obedient. They had better stay beside their mothers and learn how to cook, otherwise nobody will marry them.

However, I do not know whether or not you know this, but because women now have equal opportunities for education they have gradually been taking on an increasing number of jobs which were once assigned only to men. We find more and more women working as doctors, engineers, and politicians. Many women enter careers which, in the past, were allowed only for men, even though women's determination, logical and reasoning abilities, and leadership skills are equal to that of men, and always have been.

It seems as if men have not noticed that society has silently changed. Hence, most of them have still not even thought of learning to do the jobs that were traditional for women, such as caring for children and rearing them with love and patience.

This is really a terrible situation for men to be in! Becoming holistic, women now have characteristics and abilities of both sexes, and are doing the jobs which were previously only allowed to men. However, faced by fierce competition in society and the recession, men have not transformed either in mentality or capability. They have fallen into a miserable minority, complaining and being idle all day.

Therefore, the holistic gender-education of the New Age is exactly what we need to solve the problems of the future. Parents and educational staffs should keep this educational ideal in mind: treat every boy and girl as a holistic person, which means that boys should not be educated only in traditional boys' ways and girls should not be educated simply in traditional girls' ways. Boys and girls should be allowed to develop all the characteristics and abilities of both sexes. Boys must try to learn everything that girls know how to do (except giving birth to a child) and vice versa. That will ensure that the next generation may possess the characteristics of both sexes and be able to face the challenges of the future.

32. THE MYTH OF GENDER.

Teenagers often suffer when they discover that their sexual orientation, creativity, abilities, and traits do not fit the gender roles which they are expected to have. The pressures toward conformity coming from parents, peers, or society, only serve to make teenagers uncertain about their humanity, and to no longer believe in themselves.

The society of the past was very simple. Personal roles and identities, mental traits, abilities and the choice of occupation were determined by the person's sex; that is, men served as breadwinners and women served as housekeepers. Men were active, strong, resolute, powerful, and protective; women were gentle, soft, considerate, and intuitional, and at the same time, delicate. After a child was born, its entire soul, ability, and personality traits were gradually molded to fit the stereotypes of its sex. The differences between male and female came from the definition given by tradition, society, and family.

In Seth's book "The Nature of the Psyche," he recounts the gender issue precisely and inspiringly. In fact, our souls are very exuberant, and include both male and female characteristics and abilities. Our souls are always changing, they are flexible. They are not limited to one particular sex but they fuse feminine and masculine characteristics together.

We are all complete individuals who may randomly draw any characteristics and abilities, either masculine or feminine, from our soul's store of knowledge. The nature of the psyche is bisexual, and all relationships and interactions are based on bisexual connections. However, how may we explain the obvious physical differences and sex hormones that make men and women different?

First, the only basic difference between all males and females is the ability to give birth. Mature men provide healthy sperm in order to fertilize the ova in mature women's wombs to provide the next wonderful generation of humanity. By doing so, genetic diversity guarantees humans the ability to engage the ever-changing environment of the world and to survive. Hence, the attraction of opposite sexes and the sex-drive after adolescence arouses a powerful desire in humans.

If that drive could easily be conquered by philosophy, morality, or religion, would humans not be exposed to the possibility of extinction at any time? Sexuality is the spiritual expression of the human body. It is meant to build intimacy among people and, in the intimate harmonization of spirit and body, people generate offspring.

Here Seth humorously said that if the aim of every session of intercourse were to produce an infant, then humanity's population would have overflowed before the dawn of civilization. Sexual activities are also to be enjoyed; they are expressions of enthusiasm.

What about homosexuals? The sexual activity between gays and lesbians cannot yield children. Does that violate human nature? Actually, in times of overpopulation and peace, the phe-

nomenon of, and issues related to, homosexuality gradually surface. There is no need for a population crisis. The goal here is for
people to face and integrate the bisexual traits inside themselves.
This tends to break the old shackles of sex-roles and to release
the potential and creativity of the human soul.

Second, the physical differences of both genders and different expressions of masculinity and femininity triggered by
inherited messages aid in the soul's development in the area of
sexuality. However, you must understand that this development
is only a reference, a convenience, not an innate limitation, reg-
ulation, or acquired societal frame. If that great soul of yours, an
exuberant and flexible soul, had to force itself into a contradictory and unaccommodating gender role, rather than expressing
its completeness and richness, the ensuing pain would become
apparent.

This is also why modern people delay their marriages.
They think instinctually that they do not want to enter the traditional family life with its sexual stereotypes. Who says that
men have to be the breadwinners and women have to stay at
home mopping the floor, cooking, and caring for the children?

The creativity and nature of the soul is directly in conflict
with traditional sexual roles. Teenagers often suffer when they
discover that their sexual orientation, creativity, abilities, and
traits do not fit the gender roles that they are expected to have.
In other words, it is as if a man who does not think himself masculine enough, or a woman who doubts herself as an incomplete
woman are not human beings!

Therefore, thoroughly understanding the bisexual nature
of humans and breaking the excessive sexual boundaries and

artificial divisions will lessen the chaos in society. To release a lively and creative soul from the shackles of gender-roles is what helps us to achieve greatness and richness of the soul. An ideal like this should be prescribed as the guide for educating our next generation, with the hope of cultivating healthy, happy, and creative offspring.

33. CHILDREN'S HEARTS, PARENTS' LOVE.

Many parents ask me "How should I help my child if he lacks confidence?"

First, we should learn one thing: Never treat lack of confidence as a problem. This will make children feel that they are a problem. We should help children to understand that the lack of confidence is only temporary; it is a common psychological phenomenon experienced by many people. After giving the children confirmation, we can take a further step to lead them. Those who have attended group psychotherapy sessions tell us that people often sympathize with those with conditions similar to theirs; this gives them a sense of comfort.

In the competitive environment of studying, many parents worry that if their children have low grades, they will probably lose their self-confidence and have difficulties in the future. However, sometimes the children who lack self-confidence are not the ones who have bad grades.

In fact, the children who meet their parents' expectations and perform well, may have become accustomed to filling their empty hearts with external performances and accomplishments. Thus, they are prone to psychological problems; while those who do not have such expectations face less pressure and blame, have healthier minds.

Whether or not a child will succeed in the future should be estimated based on how much frustration he or she can endure. Real success will come to the ones who can meet failure and who are brave enough to try regardless of the frustration. Those people who act gingerly and are afraid to make mistakes will pass away from society very easily.

However, educationally, parents still need to enculturate their children according to their nature. You should help them change their disadvantages into the motivations which spur them to grow. By returning their sovereignty, you can allow them to learn how to assume responsibility for their own behavior.

When many parents are dealing with parenthood's issues, they have many worries. They are afraid that children will become annoyed if they nag them too much. Scolding them may be copied. To teach or not to teach, that is the question. Actually, when adults take an opposing position to children and preach to them or try to correct them, it usually has little effect. Instead, they should first accept the message behind the children's behavior and confirm it with them. Then they will lower their guard and open the door to communication.

Let us look at this example: some families are always performing "shows" of sibling rivalry. For instance, when the family had only one child, he had all of his parents' care and love until, one day, his brother was born. The first child's love became divided. The older child would always take the opportunity to bully his younger brother behind their parents' backs by hitting him or offending him to get him annoyed.

I think that when facing this situation, the parents should first empathize with the older child or be a spectator, while secretly helping the younger one who was bullied. They should not hastily punish the older son, for he will think that his younger brother is the reason he is has been scolded and fallen out of favor. This may make him hit his brother even more fiercely afterwards.

To examine this situation more deeply, let's return to the nature of love. What is love? Why do people not feel enough of it? If parents are perceived by the elder child as expressing less love toward him than for his younger brother, he will blame his brother for this. From a mental and physical perspective, if the parents are able to help their child to understand that, in some situations, what the boy gets is freedom, independence, and trusting love; even though they cannot always be paying attention to him, he will not feel scared and lost. Hence, he will not think he has to fight for the love he thought he had lost because of the appearance of his younger brother.

Whenever parents scold their children, the children know only that they are being punished. They do not understand that their parents' intention is "We're doing everything for your own good." We should first assure the children that their parental love definitely prevails despite their demands and expectations. If children absorb this message, then when the parents become elderly, react tardily, and gain bad habits, they might also scold their parents for the same reason "We're doing everything for your good. Seth has said, "Even for a better goal, we cannot rationalize our means." Once the children feel their parents' love, their behavior will naturally be changed.

If you thought of children as beings living within your heart, how would you treat them? To some degree, how we treat our children reflects how we treat ourselves. Perhaps parents should ask themselves first: "Do I allow myself not to do a good job or to make mistakes?" When teaching children, our ideas must be flexible. Sometimes you must see the world from a child's point of view, and also allow your children to see things from your perspective. You will learn that children are actually mature and intelligent.

34. PROBLEM CHILDREN AND MARITAL CRISIS.

During my childhood my mother often said things like: "We might have divorced at that time if it were not for you!" However, everyone knows that elders like to complain; children are not sure whether they are telling the truth. Is it possible that parents chose not to divorce for the sake of their children?

In my psychiatric department, I often meet bothered parents. I remember there was one child who constantly got himself into trouble at school. He skipped classes, stole, and humiliated the teacher with a group of people (teenagers will use the term "dis"). This meant his parents were frequently going to his school. They apologized to the teacher, pleaded for the forgiveness of their son with other parents, and paid the medical fees of other children (because their own darling always hit other classmates for trifling reasons).

The parents came come to my clinic sighing. They were totally cooperating with each other for the sake of their child.

After a thorough conversation, I learned the parents had had marital problems since the beginning of their marriage. The wife wanted a divorce the day after the marriage because she thought her husband had cheated on her. Not only did her husband's bad habits like gambling and drinking all come to the surface, but also her husband's family had many unreasonable demands.

However, as the proverb goes, heaven does not abide by the wishes of people; the idea of divorcing had been suppressed because she was pregnant. After their child was born, and for a decade after, as the child gradually grew, the parents fought all the time and their home always had a tense atmosphere. But the wife still thought she couldn't leave her husband and child, who was still very young.

Finally, the child entered junior high school. The wife then thought she could eventually end the marriage, and, in fact, she formally got a divorce. But nobody suspected that a problem child had appeared.

Indeed, in clinical cases, this situation is quite common. Familial education experts often suggest that children are the scapegoats in problematic families; problematic marriages produce a great number of children with behavioral and emotional problems. But this scapegoating is not completely correct.

Any child's problems or symptoms must have a positive meaning and this is what we should keep in mind when we are helping problem children. Like the example mentioned previously, the child had already known there were some problems in his parents' marriage and he grew up with an underlying sense of insecurity and uncertainty.

After he entered junior high school, even though his

mother said nothing, he knew his mother desperately wanted a divorce. The child's subconscious was full of insecurity. He feared having a broken family, his parents divorcing, and him becoming an orphan. His parents seemed to fight from dawn until dusk; otherwise, they refused to talk to each other.

The child did not know how to express his fear well. (Will anyone listen?) Hence, many bad behaviors at school such as fighting, cursing, and rebelling are "SOS's"—somebody please come! Who can help me? Fears fill my heart. I need someone to care about me, understand me, and listen to me, but all my parents do all day is quarrel. And they are almost divorced. My mom is leaving us. What can I do?

Children's problematic behaviors are aimed at drawing attention, seeking care and help. But some teachers who do not understand this only punish and blame the child for disturbing the learning of the whole class. Under these circumstances, the children will no doubt worsen. Ha! And then one day, children's problems finally get the attention of the parent because teachers, other parents, or representatives from law enforcement start to approach them. Ha! The problems of the children finally overtake the parents' marital problems.

The child with the problems forces the parents to ignore their marital crisis temporarily and drop the decision of divorcing. By becoming the parents' common enemy, children make their parents think no more of being each other's enemy. The problem children make the parents who do not communicate have one more chance to fight together. For the sake of their children, together they ask the teacher for help, sit together and talk to the experts, cry together, worry together, and even share the same room once again. In other words, the children construct for themselves problems to prevent their parents from divorcing, to stop the family from being broken, and to prevent themselves from becoming children in single-parent families.

If you ask any one of the children, is it worthwhile to do so? 99% of them will definitely yell that it is not only worthwhile, but it is a bargain. Therefore, in a clinic for teenagers, I often assist the worrying parents and understand that the child is stopping their parents from divorcing via his behavioral and emotional problems. By becoming the common problem of their parents, they make their parents "learn together" again.

Life is very amazing. Sometimes the appearance of a problem is meant to prevent another, bigger problem from happening. Hence, when we solve problems, we should not only see the bad effects of that problem but sometimes we should ponder: Can there be a positive result of this problem?

35. TRUSTING ONE'S GROWTH ENVIRONMENT.

Many psychologists stress the fact that our family environment has the most influence in our lives. The health of our personality is largely decided by the early stages of rearing and how our parents nurture us.

Surely, in my clinic, many problem children, teenagers, and persons with anti-social behaviors belong to families with problems. Their parents may have a bad relationship, often argue over the teaching methods, or may even fight with each other. Perhaps, they do not get along well because one has emotional problems, alcoholism, or a mental disorder. It may be a single-parent family or a broken family with the single parent worrying about the finances, taking care of the child and overcoming his or her own pain and loneliness. Honestly, avoiding being problem children while having these kinds of familial environments is difficult.

Moreover, the pessimism of parents will deeply influence their children. Some children cannot escape the shadows of their families. The rank a child holds among siblings and how good his/her behavior is also have an influence on the child's personality and self-confidence. For instance, when a child is reared with the pressure of matching his outstanding older brothers and sisters, he sees that others are always being complimented but he is only scolded. The self-abasement resulting from this mental trauma can even influence the child's eventual marriage.

A number of theories of child development indicate that children are born to be the saviors of families. They try hard to meet their parents' expectations and do what their parents did not accomplish in order to repay their love and care. However, some children have been told by their parents every day since they were young how tough life is, how frustrating marriage is, who took advantage of them, and who looked down on them. Then they exhort their children to be promising in the future.

And. terribly, after they become adults, some children do try to live up to their parents' expectations throughout their whole lives. Although their parents did not ask them to do so, they want to accomplish in their lives what their parents were unable to do.

An interesting image is always in my mind: that of a beloved cat who always brings sparrows and mice for his master from outside. It joyfully carries them in its mouth to its master, hoping to be complimented and to repay its master's love. Children like this may never be their own selves and they never learn to love themselves or live for themselves. Their whole lives exist to repay their parents or to meet their parents' expectations.

This kind of life is really too painful. Some children will come to hate and rebel against their parents, but this is every child's deepest conflict. Children hope to be loved, for their parents to be proud of them, and to make them feel they did not rear them in vain. On the other hand, children want to have their own lives. Life is to be used for pursuing their own goals and ideals, not just to be a tool of or sources of content for their parents, which may lead potentially to a total abandonment one's self.

Older psychological theories often think of children as a family environment's victims and they blame the familial and educational environments for their mental problems. Yet this kind of thought greatly underestimates every child's spiritual capability and potential for growth.

Spiritually, all infants choose the time, country, ethnicity, sex, rearing environment, siblings, and parents they want for rebirth. All infants also know that their parents and their familial environments are custom-made for the needs and growth of their spirits in this life. In the past, you may never have encountered such viewpoints and theories, or accepted them. You would always think that you had no choice but to be placed in that awful family and sometimes you would think of yourself as a victim of the environment. However, these old ideas were not helpful to you; they only deepened your feelings of victimization and anger.

The concepts of Seth can truly help you see the potential of the spirit: You have choices. You chose a poor family because you want to learn to surpass it. You chose a miserable childhood to learn how to love, to be kind, and to have courage. Therefore, please trust your growth environment. It has been custom-made by your soul for the mercy, wisdom, and love in your life. Trust the great spiritual potential inside you and trust your own life.

36. UNCONDITIONAL LOVE.

We have always regarded the love which parents give to children as unconditional, but we seldom mention the love which children give to parents. In the psychiatric department, in many cases, I found that children's love towards their parents is truly unconditional.

Because survival is a necessity and a child's maturity must wait until cranial nerve cells grow, children fully accept and identify with their parents' values. Before children have developed self-defenses and the ability to judge reality for themselves, the adoption of their parents' beliefs creates a tight bond between children and their parents. In children's hearts, parents are God. Parents not only provide them with food, but also help them clean their bodily waste, not to mention providing security and protection from danger. Therefore, although all children are unique, their values are mostly inherited from parents because they have not developed their own independent personality and thought.

Parents' love for children is often affected by many factors such as their own mood, children's sexes, their rank among siblings, their performance, grades, and behaviors, as well as whether or not they have the ability to love. Thus, almost all the parents' love for children is conditional love.

However, children's love for parents is not the same. I have mentioned that children have not yet developed independent thought and sensibility. Thus, to children, parents are the only reliable persons in their lives. Parents satisfy all of their needs; therefore, children must trust and love their parents 100% because they cannot live without their parents' protection and provision, or their trust and love.

In other words, the unconditional trust and love that children have for their parents is necessary for them to survive and it is mentally essential. It will not be polluted by rational thinking and reality. Rather, it is a kind of bond combined with emotional trust and values. For instance, children will not decide whether or not to love their parents according to their parents' degree, temper, or earning ability. Children will be influenced by those factors only after they reach adulthood and have their own thinking and judgment. No matter what, each child's love for parents is complete.

Children's full love for parents and unconditional acceptance of their values has many functions. Emotionally, it is meant to be the deepest promise. Through the feeling of full love in life, no matter how much frustration, failure, and indifference children will face in adulthood, they can still feel the warmth of full love deep in their hearts. As a matter of sensibility, it is fundamental to the development of children's personalities.

First, children accept their parents' view of the universe, of life, and of the children to help them while they are being reared.

When they eventually gain their own independent thought and mature actions, they decide how many thoughts from their parents which have been indoctrinated and influenced in them should remain. They also see other viewpoints by learning from their peers, books, or the media. This is the period that we call "teenage rebellion."

Teenage rebellion is an important time when children influence whether their adult lives will be mentally healthy. It is also a time when children are delicate, emotional, and need the most help. However, sometimes parents give little help to adolescents and they even make it worse for them. Teenagers want to rid themselves of the perspectives inherited during childhood and build their independence and power.

On the one hand, they want to keep their privacy and build their independent thinking. On the other hand, they intensely oppose their parents and retreat from the old-fashioned ideas which they dislike. Parents, facing their rebellious children, are often busy with their own work. How can they help their children resolve their internal conflicts and build a healthy and normal personality? That is why parents often think their kids have changed and they can feel a tear in the love.

Some parents' personalities are not mature enough, so they want their children to give up their independent personalities and values in order to keep their love bond strong. Thus, children are under great pressure. They are afraid of losing their parents' love after they become independent or that they will break their parents' hearts. To maintain their bond, they abandon and sacrifice their independent thinking and integrity, thus causing many mental disorders: melancholia, schizophrenia, and manic-depressive psychosis.

Hence, it is very important to help children to build a healthy rebellious phase and complete their maturation, which is based on the parents' unconditional love. However, if parents overly protect, excessively interfere with, overly criticize, worry too much about, and apply their own values to children because they have fears, saying, "Child, I have experienced more than you; child, just do what I say, or you'll definitely do wrong or get hurt," they will rear children who never mature or are rebellious and abnormal children.

Give children love. Respect their thoughts and choices while they are maturing. Do not protect and interfere excessively. These are the correct ways to educate children.

* * *

PART 4: RECOVERING THE INNOCENT HEART

Children are our inner heart's own children;

Children remind us of the intimate interaction of our spirits with nature;

Children tell us that time does not exist and it may be created by our spirit;

Children show us that life is simple and joyous;

Children are the "Natural face of God" in our hearts.

Perhaps, what children bring us is far more truthful and useful than what we want to teach them.

37. AWAKENING THE SPIRITUAL LAND.

True learning should awaken the spiritual realm inside children, and should inspire children's subjective feelings and abundant imagination, to make them feel that nature does in fact emerge from the "spiritual world." Only with this kind of teaching and learning can we make people get closer to their own spirits and to nature's heart.

We rarely pay attention to children's dreams, but dreams are important in determining their learning development.

As early as infants learn how to crawl, they already play games involving walking and running in their dreams. This kind of game, which simply involves muscle activity, brings infants great pleasure, challenge, and a sense of accomplishment. They are already familiar with the important techniques of how to crawl and walk; thus, crawling and walking in real life is not at all strange to them. They stride confidently forward in life because all of these skills which they learned, and the children may be assured of in their dreams. There is no reason to be afraid!

However, learning in dreams is not confined to physical acts; concepts are also presented. Do you think children encounter mathematical concepts only after they enter kindergarten or elementary school? Wrong! Actually, children have one type of dream which especially stimulates their mathematical knowledge. In this type of dream, children play with numbers as if playing a game. They see how addition, subtraction, multiplication, and division generate different numbers and results. That is right, the mathematical formulas are not carved in the children's brains, but the "mathematical equations" are included in our neural structures when we are born; spatial and geometric concepts are not extrinsic. This is a natural consequence of when our brains, essentially duplicates of our minds, play games with space, figures, and lines.

When we teach mathematics and geometry to children, we should not necessarily ask them to learn the formulas by heart. Instead, we should use games, which can help them to recall the origin of the formulas. During this process, children gradually remember what they learned in the dreams. With this guidance, which incorporates the understanding of innateness and dreams, children are able to learn with joy and know more about themselves, but are not forced to learn those solid formulas which have nothing to do with them.

Children's knowledge of science does not come exclusively from textbooks. An infant born on a plain may never see the mountains or the sea. However, human psyches naturally have an adequate understanding of the earth's environment. In the unconscious spiritual environment, children keep gaining knowledge about mountains, hills, plains, and seas which is not merely a literal realization but more like a direct spiritual experience. When a child first sees the sea or touches its waves, he has a special familiarity—this is how it feels to touch it with one's hands and see the sea with one's eyes. This strong sensory experience has indescribable beauty. It also evokes the kindness in the child's spirit to unite with the sea.

Nowadays, the most prominent method for educating children is a kind of "outward-facing learning," which closes off both the lively spiritual energy in their inner selves and many of the direct spiritual experiences from their dreams. True learning should awaken the spiritual world inside children and inspire children's innate subjective feelings and abundant imaginations, and make children feel that the whole of nature does in fact emerge from the "spiritual world." Only with this kind of teaching and learning may people get closer to their own spirits and nature's heart.

When a child first sees a rose, he laughs happily and respectfully. He feels that the rose is not merely a flower growing from the soil. Not only can he appreciate the beauty of the rose with his naked eyes, smell its aroma, and touch its spiky stem, but also, most importantly, he feels that there is a mysterious connection between his feelings and the rose. He knows instinctively that there is a sacred bond between the rose's origin and his own. He smiles, not just because of his joy, but, more so: a joyful smile which is mysterious, solemn, kind, and sacred to nature.

Maybe this child does not have the knowledge of a botanist. Botanists have in their minds the scientific names of flowers, their colloquial names, types, origins, and distributions. They may be knowledgeable about their backgrounds and gene mappings. But, honestly, they do not "know" the rose better than children do. When a child sees the rose, he breaks into a smile. In that smile, without speaking, it has already revealed all the secrets of heaven and earth.

Children's life experiences are direct and intense. Perhaps adults have more knowledge or information than children, but they have already forgotten the natural intimacy they had when they first met heaven and earth. The more we seem to learn and the more intelligent we become, the more we are isolated from ourselves and from nature.

Therefore, Seth emphasizes repeatedly recalling how your heart raced when you saw the ocean and the rose for the first time. When we truly go deep into our subjective feelings, every intimate experience in life that appears to be normal actually contains the mystery of the whole universe.

38. PLAYING GAMES WITH TIME.

Children experience time in a way which adults have forgotten. Adults seem to be tied to a "time train" which departs from the past, goes through the present and heads for the unpredictable future. This train will fade as time passes and disappears at the terminal. However, children's minds, when they awaken after dreaming or making good use of their inner senses, can still feel the great flexibility of their consciousnesses. As a result, while they are playing, they can play recklessly with time.

For example, I am not sure whether people notice that although fairy tales always start with "Once upon a time..." whether it is in the past or future is not important to children. This does not imply that children have no concept of the past or the future. Instead, from their perspective, both the past and the future happen "in the present moment." Therefore, children's games always take place "in the moment." Whether in the distant past or the imagined future, children's minds always pull it to the present. They experience the "past" and "future" through the present. While they do so, children's imaginations, minds, and physical senses can break through the barrier of time. They can indeed arouse extrasensory perception and glimpse events which happened in the past or may occur in the future through the present.

Children's ability to play games with time is akin to the "inner senses" described by Seth. Each person's innate inner senses can lead us to break through the boundaries of time and space. We can have a direct experience of the "spacious present" including the "moments" of the past, the present, and the future. The physical senses which we use the most now are prepared by our inner souls. We use them to feel physical phenomena.

However, the material civilization of human beings has developed to a critical point. Our spiritual capabilities and inner senses need to be opened gradually. Only with the emergence of a spiritual civilization may we recover from our unbalanced material civilization.

Adults are familiar with their consciousness's manipulation of the material world. The children's games are often related to the passage of time. For example, a six-year-old child will not only imagine what he will be like in thirty years but truly experience his mind thirty years in the future and experiences the "future" at that moment. When he pretends that he is thirty-six years old, he enters his own thirty-six-year-old memory. He becomes the person who he will be thirty years later in the "spacious present." This may be difficult for adults to imagine but, to the children, it seems that they really wear the future thirty-six-year-old body and engage the thirty-six-year-old mind. But when his mother calls him, he will return to the present—a six-year-old child.

Playing games with time enriches children's spirits and real experiences. Children often look to the past and experience the future spontaneously through the games they are playing at any given moment. In other words, the moment is the locus of children's power. Do we not often discover that children may not own many things but they are easily satisfied mentally? A plan to go hiking tomorrow may make them happy all day long.

Comparatively, adults have more time, money, and resources but they lose their ability to play games with time and space because of the gradual diminishment of their imaginations. Being unable to escape, they are stuck in the immutable reality.

Imaginations are the wings of the soul. In a comfortable room with a normal temperature, children can play so vividly that they are able to imagine themselves freezing on the polar ice cap, having goosebumps, and eventually being as frozen as a popsicle. On the one hand, they may become engrossed in the imagined and "present" games. They may even feel a drop in their body temperature, the slowing of their circulation, and the blunting of their consciousness. On the other hand, they know well that they are in a normal environment.

However, as people mature, they worry that their imaginations will bring their consciousness too far, and be afraid of departing from reality. As a result, adults start to quell their own imaginations, stuck in the "present" of time and space. Moreover, people's fear of time increases day by day as if it is a merciless killer. On the contrary, instead of shortening our lives, time enriches the content of them. The conclusion is that you should start to learn from children how to play games with time.

If these are the "dog days of summer," try to imagine a colorful spring before your eyes. If you are now forty years of age, play games with time by pretending you are an eight-year-old or an eighty-year-old when you are free to see whether your subjective feelings or real experiences differ. Through this process, you may realize something new and break through the limits of time and space, and enter a different phase of your life.

39. CREATIVE ROLE-PLAYING.

To children, being awake and asleep dreaming are both parts of playing. They experiment with everything and play every single role with their powerful imaginations and creativity. Children have neither the many preconceived notions nor limited thinking that adults have. They understand that the past events of our lives and our destinies are all "plastic." Everything may happen this way or that, and may create this ending or that consequence.

Games played by children in their daily lives naturally extend their learning in their dreams.

In children's dreams, they may dream of themselves as their own fathers, mothers, brothers, sisters, the cats they kept, mosquitoes, or soldiers. When they awaken, they then begin to "role-play" in a game which they had started independently. They take turns playing each of the roles and learn which ones suit them and which ones do not in a short time. Through continuous role-playing, they recognize who they are and "the rules of the game" for the real world.

Children are full of imagination, which makes them unlimited by adult "rules of the game" and fixed roles. They do their best to expand the flexibility of their consciousnesses, and continue imitating and pretending. In their own games, they imitate their parents' arguments. They take turns playing the roles of the one who loses his temper and screams or the one crying sorrowfully. Through this process, they can realize how people in this situation feel. Furthermore, they can realize more deeply the dramatic tension of the interaction of various roles.

Children do not excessively identify with their own identities, sexes, ages, and life experiences. They will portray themselves as everything which exists around them. For example, children are able to see themselves and their bedrooms from a desk's perspective. By looking at himself from the desk's perspective, the child feels his own mood and talks to himself.

When a child encounters an animal which he has never previously seen and does not know how to react to, he will imitate the animal's behavior. By pretending to be that animal, the child finds out how that animal usually reacts and then teaches himself how to face this reaction.

Thus, children play games with their consciousnesses in way adults have forgotten. They try to portray all the characters existing around them in order to learn. In the process of role-playing and learning, they identify their own feelings one by one and imagine the external world's feedback.

For instance, they will soon learn that when they pretend to be flies or bad children, almost all the reactions they receive will be negative. The fluidity of a child's consciousness enables him easily to become anyone around him, to feel how the others feel, and even to view himself from the perspective of another. In other words, besides a child's self-recognition, there is a larger "gestalt of consciousness." By imitating and pretending to be others, children know what "others" are, and know that they are not "the others" but "themselves." Thus, they strengthen their unique identities.

During dreams, a child's mind will create all possible versions of an event based on a specific one. During everyday games, children's performances are quite different from reality. For example, a single-parent child will often role-play how he gets along with his brothers, sisters, and parents spontaneously in order to create a diverse learning environment. However, this spiritually spontaneous learning behavior is often not only discouraged but often forbidden by the parents lest the child should stray from reality. Nevertheless, if a child's imagination could not envision other realities, how would he be able to see more clearly, and adapt to, his "official" reality?

As mentioned earlier, children do not have preconceived ideas like adults do. Anything can happen. They have a specific and delicate way of experimenting with possible versions of each event, and choose those which most closely match their true nature. Playing is life, and vice versa. Adults have already forgotten that it is indeed the correct attitude to take towards life.

Speaking frankly, family life is also a kind of "role-playing." Someone plays Dad, someone plays Mom, and someone plays the Child. Just like children play with dolls, the family members use exaggeration and drama to reveal the essence and true meaning of their lives.

In fact, life itself is a vivid role-playing affair. You are the role which your inner "divine self" plays. Nevertheless, do not forget that you are one of the many roles played by your "divine self." Your life is one of the possible scenarios which your "divine self" may play. "You" are far "bigger" than your role and your life, and you are also unlimited. Therefore, when you do not like your own role and your life, remember that life itself is a game. You can use a highly creative sense of play trying out different roles and life stories.

Remember, the role-playing games which one plays as a child could really help you, also. You can be yourself or pretend to be others equally well and learn to transcend your present role and thus change your life.

40. THE MEANING BEHIND ILLNESS.

Fevers, coughs, asthma, various cancers (especially leukemia), intestinal viral infections which infect a group, headaches, and stomach aches. What do these diseases mean to children? How do children's spirits view these diseases? Do diseases represent, to some extent, the difficulties from which they want to flee?

To adults, diseases represent an unwelcome health condition caused by the invasion of our bodies by foreign microbes. They have to be a malfunctioning of our bodies, or the result of the mutation of our chromosomes. They must happen because the environmental threat is so great and the body's immune system is so weak, that they all need assistance from medical science.

How do children's spirits view these diseases? What do these diseases mean to children?

First, children know much more than adults do about the relation between their body and spirit. I call this the "united body and mind." And, children are quite aware of this on a conscious level. They use their willingness to make themselves ill in order to get themselves out of difficulties.

Children will react intensively to people, events, and things they do not like. However, they are only children, and they do not have much freedom or autonomy. They are often locked in a situation where they are forced to do everything they are told to do. But they know innately the causal connection between their minds and their health. They know that the functioning of their bodies will change with their minds. In fact, this is not the limit of children's psyches!

Basically, they know the cooperative relation between themselves and germs. When necessary, children's psyches will activate those inactive microbes which have been hiding in their bodies or they will "invite" germs from outside to invade and, meanwhile, lower the defenses of their bodies. This makes them ill in order to satisfy some of their needs.

From what kinds of difficulties will children try to escape? At home, it may be a lack of affection or companionship. Children learn swiftly that sickness can help them obtain extra attention and affection. It may be that the parents are too strict and hit them often. There is no doubt that being ill will protect them from the fear of being blamed. It might be that at first the child's parents argue all day and the family is on the border of collapsing. At this time, a child's fatal leukemia makes the family harmonious and the parents having to alternate in keeping the child company day and night. "Getting a divorce?" Not a chance!

At school, children want to escape from many things: a teacher who demands, hits, scolds, and scares them; classmates who bully, laugh at, and hurt them; a subject which scares them (e.g. memorizing multiplication tables or reciting poetry).You see, children have really sensitive hearts and the influence of a group of people is extremely strong. If they play too much, stopping is difficult.

Let us look at intestinal infections, for example: When the collective fear of a group of children is aroused, and they are intensified by parents' worries, and there is a temptation not to attend school, then the "cooperative adventure" of the children's collective psyche and the intestinal infection unfolds. Relative to a child's great psychic strength, this manipulation is a piece of cake, but these situations actually scare the adults so much that they prepare to take serious action. However, to children, this kind of experience contains elements of fun, games, and adventure.

This point of view does not mean that an intestinal virus

does not need to be cured or prevented, or that it is simply a practical joke of children or that nobody will be killed. It is not! What I mean is that I hope people will have a wider and more open mind. Do not be deceived by the surface reality of the intestinal infection, but look more deeply into that reality, understand the creativity of children's minds, the importance of their will, and the accumulation of fear. These factors are more important in causing the formation of a disease and the outbreak of a collective infection than merely the combined existence of viruses, the effect of the environment, and factors inside the body. People simply did not know that in the past!

Therefore, here is the important question. Because children have the great power of their psychic creativity (which adults have already forgotten) and they can also heal themselves with their willingness, should we be constantly indoctrinating them with theories like "viruses cause disease" or "physical conditions, the environment, and genes cause disease?" Should we be leading them to believe in objective medical procedures, and make them forget their psychic creativity, the ability to cooperate with viruses, that "they cause their own sickness," and, most unfortunately of all, "how to heal themselves with will-power"?

Hence, children gradually lose their psychic creativity and become adults with delicate physical conditions and little immunity to diseases (SARS, cancer, chronic disease, AIDS). Meanwhile, while medical technology develops, more people become ill and they are more difficult to cure. Dear readers, is this situation what you want? Let us teach children to understand their psychic creativity and guide them to develop their self-healing ability!

41. THE LITTLE PSYCHIC MAGICIAN.

In general, children are closer to their own spirits more than most of adults are to theirs, and they also better understand the creativity of the soul.

For instance, children innately have the power to make themselves ill. Some parents are too busy with their business, and thus take less care of their kids, or make the children feel their parents' love is not directed towards them. This of course causes a sense of insecurity and fear in the children. So they think, "If I'm sick, Daddy and Mommy will come and hug me, stay with me, buy toys and something yummy for me." This idea will trigger the power inside the heart, which will strongly decrease the body's immunity. Thus, children can "cooperate" with viruses and germs, creating a mental atmosphere that will make themselves sick in order to really make themselves sick.

In my clinical experience, many children's cases are about the problem they have after their younger brothers and sisters are born, and they see that the adults' attention is turned toward the new member in their family and that the care they had previously has decreased. At this time, children do not see the whole picture, and thus experience a great sense of panic and insecurity. When they are fighting for toys and love, they are told: "You're the older brother; you should be nice to your little sister."

This makes the children's feeling of loss even bigger. In this state of being afraid and being unloved, children may envy their younger siblings and seek opportunities for revenge. However, this only makes the situation worse.

At this moment, children yell in their hearts "Daddy and Mommy don't love me anymore!" They are eager for their parents' love and concern once again; thus, the conscious mind and emotional motivations are again triggered. The inner psychic strength is in charge of all physical functions. When combined with inherited traits and the environment, children can soon lead the power of their minds to make them ill.

Thus, atopic dermatitis, allergic rhinitis, fever, and asthma may appear. Those parents who understand nothing, of course, will once again give to the sick children the care and love for which they are eager, and will not scold them any more. They will also take them everywhere for injections and medicine, trying various folk prescriptions to improve their children's health, but that only makes them worse.

Children's psychic strength is powerful and it moves very swiftly. They are clear in their hearts that they are like "magicians." Children innately understand the reasons for the unity of the mind-body spirit. They may not show their comprehension explicitly, but they are experienced in realizing it and they have the power to summon diseases at any time. They also understand that unless they themselves grant permission, no germs or viruses can make them ill. Each person is born with this innate ability and intuition.

Many children encounter obstacles to learning or are punished by teachers and bullied by classmates at school. Due to intense fear, they resist going to school. Usually, this fear causes the balance of microbes in the body to take only one night to become unbalanced, thus causing the normally harmless pathogens to become dangerous. The next morning, the thermometer shows that these children have a fever. This is a simple task for children.

In addition, children's psychic sensitivity and creativity are very strong. If one child contracts an infectious disease, an atmosphere of psychic terror spreads immediately, which is a great vehicle for the microbes. Hence, it erupts into a collective infection immediately. Many experts regarding infectious diseases have always thought the reason is that the power of the disease is too strong, so they begin by investigating the paths of infection and try to formulate an antibiotic. Needless to say, they totally have no idea about the role played behind the scenes by the children's collective creativity of the psyche.

As children grow, they repeatedly receive a message telling them "You're sick because of viruses and bacteria that you cannot see working. You have to wash your hands to get rid of them. You have no immunity to germs. You're sick because your immune system and body are weak, and you have to rely on medicine to be cured." Therefore, children are confused, so they gradually adopt the story promoted by adults and society. Parents, teachers, and doctors seem to know more after all. (In fact, the opposite is true.)

That is why children progressively lose their spiritual power. They cannot magically heal themselves as before. The power has been given to viruses, germs, doctors, and medicine. As a result, when we are adults, we completely forget our spiritual power and how we can make ourselves ill. Unfortunately, at the same time, we forget how to cure ourselves.

42. IMAGINING WHAT DYING IS LIKE.

Why is life full of suffering? Is it because humanity is prone to look for misery or is it really that the environment is so tough? Can we find any clues for the suffering of humanity for children's thinking and behavior?

In children's spontaneous games, they often play ones that involve "being killed," whether it is being stabbed by knives, being shot by machine guns, or imagining themselves falling from a wall, breaking their necks and wriggling on the floor. They try to imagine what it is like to die and they can vividly feel being close to death. Why are children so strange? Is it because of violent cartoons and TV programs?

To explain this phenomenon in depth, we should start from the point of reincarnation. Basically, souls come to this world to experience, as much as possible, the feelings of delight, anger, sorrow, and happiness—the depth and scope of different kinds of emotions. They also wish to sample all bodily senses: starvation, chill, exultation, sickness, etc. Thus, for souls, their earthly experience seems to be "I feel therefore I am."

By their nature, children will inherently be curious about suffering and want to know what it is like—through games and mimicking scenes from television, for they want to learn how to avoid the suffering which they dislike and help people to prevent the suffering that they do not want. In this process, what is really important is the lessons the souls have learned in order to understand every layer of emotion and feeling that they have inherited. Then, as adults, they will allow themselves to feel the reality of their own emotions and they will not cause others pain.

Not only may children experience the feeling of suffering from games, but so may many adults who are congenitally disabled or who have long suffered from diseases. The sense of feeling hurt helps people to sympathize with others. This helps to lessen some of the causes of unnecessary suffering in society.

These are some very important educational principles for children: never suppress children's direct experience of emotions (especially sadness, weakness and pain); do not ask them to pretend that they are not in pain or sad; do not force children to deny their feelings.

Teaching children to deny their direct experience of emotions or their bodies is especially harmful because, by this method of education, children will more easily hurt other people. Children really want to put themselves in other's shoes, but if they have been forced to deny their feelings, their hearts, of course, no longer have any feeling. So they project their numbness towards others and ignore their suffering.

For instance, a child who has been beaten by his alcoholic father since he was young no longer has any feeling in his heart (of course this includes emotions like sadness and being hurt) when he successfully segregates or numbs his feelings of mental and physical pain. He may even be unmoved by the wailing of a woman under his fist.

Moreover, in Nazi concentration camps soldiers obeyed the orders to torture captives. For these things to happen, the soldiers' sense of being hurt had to be numbed, restricting emotions.

Seth has always said that suffering itself does not do any good to the soul, and it is not a virtue. However, it seems that many people are still looking for suffering.

Children daydream. They dream not only about kings and queens or honored knights, but also about being a victim of tragedy. I often imagined myself stabbed by several knives, heroically sacrificed, becoming a drifting corpse in the river and I enjoyed it very much. I don't know why, but becoming a drifting corpse gave me a weird sense of tranquility. I believe many children are happy to listen to stories of wicked stepmothers and experiencing a miserable life as much as possible. Actually, to some degree, adults do the same thing unconsciously, such as being attracted by soap operas or to movies with a lot of grief or tension.

As children or as adults, we all have a great curiosity regarding human experience. We live because we vigorously want to play a role in the drama of this world. Thus, we should teach children how to experience their lives but not to be overly involved in them. We should sense their feelings but not be entangled in pursuing suffering; we should cultivate empathy. By doing all this we can bring true happiness to individuals and to the world, replacing pain with joy.

43. THE DIFFERENCES BETWEEN THE HEROIC AND THE ORDINARY.

Do you still remember your favorite childhood cartoons? Do you remember Tranzor Z, G-Force, Superman, Spiderman, Teenage Mutant Ninja Turtles, and Vicky the Viking? These cartoons satisfy children's tendency towards heroism.

Each child has a hero inside his heart, with a small wish to help the world and rescue human beings. Each soul which comes to be reborn knows that it has a mission to complete. It is here to help itself and the world. At the same time, it is here to accomplish the great expansion of human consciousness.

Seth has a very good point: We are not here to bemoan human suffering; we are here to learn that if we dislike this world, we can change it with the happiness, power, and vigor in our hearts. What we need to do is to recreate in our bodies our spirits as faithfully and beautifully as we can.

This is why cartoons and comics which emphasize humanity's heroic traits strongly attract children. They also remind them that, apart from working for a living and living expenses, they have a goal which surpasses individual lives and fulfills the whole world. The inherent sanctity of life and heroism leads many children to step into their life's journey with an indescribable inspiration and trust, as well as to become cheerful and mature.

What else can be more meaningful than a life's goal of helping humans and saving the world?

However, children's hopes for heroic journeys start to collapse—first, because they are confronted with the Big Bang Theory, and its ideas about the origin of life, and second, because of Darwin's Theory of Evolution—thus completely destroying children's heroic dreams.

According to modern science, the universe was formed by a Big Bang, and the origin of life was an "accidental" spark made by the collision of molecules. Scientists do not discuss souls, but how our bodies evolved from single-celled organisms, all the way to apes, to Homo Erectus, and then to us humans.

From this perspective, humans are the tools of survival for selfish genes. Where is the greatness? Humans are merely piles of bones and flesh. Where are the heroes? How about high-mind-edness? These are just myths that humans invent to console themselves. Heroes are simply successful murderers who destroy other races simply for their own glory or to survive.

While children are still maturing, they think that their parents are heroes, immortal and flawless. Thus, they strive to become flawless in order to prove that their parents are right. This is a big burden for all children. One day, children suddenly realize their parents can become hurt, fall ill, and die. They also have their own weaknesses and make mistakes. The children are frightened, but this turns out to be the beginning of true maturity.

When children learn to think and judge for themselves, they are surprised to learn that the world of adults is completely different from what they imagined. A poor child who did not study much may become the President, a doctor, or the CEO of a large company. However, all adults must worry about being self-sufficient and handling mundane affairs.

So, where do the children's heroic journeys and personality traits go? The world that children enter upon maturity is actually very ordinary. Each person can struggle only for oneself or, at most, for their relatives. The parents whom children once thought were wonderful become ordinary couples when the children have grown.

Because of this discovery, many teenagers feel extremely lost. On the one hand, they know their souls have a great mission and they have heroic characteristics. On the other hand, they feel that these characteristics have been demolished by the belief system of modern science. Even worse, the great inner drive of their souls does not have any way to enter this adult world.

Thus, some teenagers fall into an internal conflict. Either they choose suicide to protest the ordinary world of adults that enervates their talented souls or cripples their sacred heroic traits rather than enter the boring adulthood in which people only have one aim—to live.

How many sparks can this kind of life ignite and how much meaning to life can it bring? No wonder all adults in the world are unhappy, for their heroic journeys have already been truncated in their childhoods.

The spirit of Seth stresses that life is a sacred creation of the soul and did not arise from a random collision of particles. And that human bodies are material manifestations of dream bodies, and are not evolved from apes. Each soul that comes to earth, the children who are born and live, are here to surmount their own challenges in life and to help improve humanity and the world. In this way, we can support our children's heroic journeys and recall the heroic impulse in our own adult hearts. Thus, to believe our lives are extraordinary is the greatest moment of accomplishment for our soul!

44. THE GREAT CURIOSITY.

Consciousness has far more fluidity than we have previously understood. Most people nowadays identify themselves completely with their bodies, remembering only the experiences that consciousness enacts through the body, but forgetting the actions done outside their body. Therefore, people have always thought that when the body is here, the person is here; when the body is gone, the person is gone.

However, the relationship humans had with their bodies in the past is totally different from that of modern humans. To them, the consciousness was to the body as a bird is to the nest. Doubtlessly, when birds rest in their nests, they have a sense of warmth and security. However, they may leave the nest and freely soar at any time for further experiences.

A bird will not think of itself dying when it loses its nest, but modern men believe their consciousnesses dies following the deaths of their bodies. They believe that consciousness has to work through the body, which is totally opposite to the truth.

The consciousness of early humans had great fluidity. It was not wholly kept inside the body. As Seth put it, "He realizes that he is the same rather inside or outside the body." For instance, in a cave, a mother who is sewing animal pelts together for clothing may not have been able to watch her child playing under the tree far away, but the consciousness of early humans had the ability to divide whenever necessary.

The mother would separate part of her consciousness to combine cooperatively with that of the tree so that she may simultaneously sew the clothing and watch her child from the tree's perspective. When the child returns to the mother, her consciousness would thank the tree. The consciousness of early humans had frequent and close cooperation with all animals, plants, and minerals. They were always grateful to the protective power of Mother Nature.

Early humans not only soaked their feet in the cool river

but also spontaneously divided part of their consciousnesses to join that of the water. One part of their consciousness would walk along the riverbank via their feet; the other part of it joyfully combined with the water's consciousness. As the river flowed, they could sense the view on the banks, the speed of the river, its depth, and even the living creatures in the water and on the bank.

On the one hand, early humans knew they were themselves; on the other hand, they could fully experience a part of their consciousness leaving to combine with others. For example, when a child was curious about what a tree was and how it transported water and nutrition to the treetop, he "became" the tree, with his consciousness drifting in. In other words, he realized his "treeness."

This kind of great curiosity is based on love, which is the mysterious power which allows consciousness to flow and unites everything. The fluidity of love is actually that of consciousness. Early children distinguished between "being a tree" and "being a human" by their love and curiosity for trees. They knew that trees transported water and nutrition to every leaf through tiny pipes. Although they did not know those pipes were what botanists call vascular bundles, their consciousnesses understood this fact through combining themselves with the trees.

You would not dissect your beloved pet just to learn how its heart worked, simply out of curiosity. Early humans would not damage nature in order to understand it. Seth had a very good point. When we employ research methods such as dissection and experimentation, we may understand only dead nature and never find the heart of it.

When we seek to understand animals and plants or the causes of human diseases by using experiments and dissecting, we can find only the most superficial reasons for physical changes, but the true cause may never be found!

To truly understand and do research on nature and the causes of all human diseases, we definitely cannot understand it even by using the most advanced instruments or by experimenting on animals or humans. These methods cannot really help us. In fact, the best and the most scientific research tool is one's consciousness, which has been granted to everyone.

Understanding the consciousness of early humans can re-arouse this mental bequeathment in modern humans. Humans love humans; humans love nature; nature loves humans. The power of love, which carries a strong curiosity, may again arouse within the consciousness of modern humans. In the future, humans may not need to dissect birds to understand the biomechanics of their flying, but will simply combine part of their consciousness with that of the flying birds to truly feel their flight mechanics.

Modern children to some degree are more akin to the early humans: intense love and great curiosity flow in their minds. Sometimes, their consciousness really flows and becomes part of the environment. This is a natural ability of a child's psyche to learn about the world.

However, nowadays, lamentably, these abilities within the consciousness of children will too soon be ignored and suppressed. Thus, the education of the psyche and the cultivation of conscious abilities are very important.

45. INSPIRED BY THE INNER SPIRITUAL STRENGTH.

From the bodily, spiritual, and mental points of view, each child's life does not start at the moment when he or she is born, but it is the beginning of the life of this incarnation. Each new-born baby is actually an elder; an ancestor from two or three generations before us who comes to this world through reincarnation. Thus, all parents understand that children nowadays learn very swiftly compared to themselves when they were little.

Each child is very intelligent and has his own unique perspective and notions.

As Seth put it, if each child was a piece of blank paper and had to learn from the very beginning, civilization might still be at the stage of the cavemen. Children's souls have accumulated innumerable experiences and skills. Although a whole new person has come to this world, this person is built on everything he had learned in previous incarnations. Additionally, his learning in this life may always access and reclaim all the abilities and experiences attained in the past.

Hence, there is almost never either an educational method or a method to inspire children's potential which considers how to open one's spiritual potential, including all accumulated experiences, skills, wisdom, and love (these are only part of the soul's potential) from the past ten to one hundred lifetimes. Few people are aware of the magnificence of the human mind, and understand thoroughly that, through their instincts and acquired training, each child can attain the great psychic ability to transcend time and space.

This educational method is not an impossible dream. As the New Age approaches, more and more children are born on the earth, I believe, whose souls which are here with a mission. They are brave. They had training before they came here and they understood the challenges that they would encounter on earth.

I often tell parents not to worry too much for their children's future. Society is currently in a slump. Many parents find working for a living increasingly difficult. Meanwhile they see their children not studying hard, not living up to their expectations, being immature, and not knowing how to prepare for the future. The parents worry every day that their children will not be able to compete with others in the future, or may starve.

I comfort these parents by saying this to them. When children are brave enough to come to this challenging and uncertain era, it means they were well prepared for this incarnation. They are equipped with the abilities in their hearts to engage this challenging world just as modern ships are all equipped with GPS devices. Thus, the only thing which parents and education workers can do is encourage and help the children develop their natural gifts. And we must continue to trust.

We should understand two things:

First, children are no doubt our next generation, but do not forget that they are also ancestors who have been reborn. Therefore, via education, we may help these old souls with new bodies to know themselves again, to learn their inner wisdom from thousands of years ago. We should teach as vividly and inspiringly as possible in order to help them become acquainted with various fields and subjects. And then let them move forward at full speed towards the mission of the soul. Each child will have has his own personal talent and should be cultivated individually, so he can travel along his own unique soul's road.

Second, the great potential knowledge and experience of one's mind neither comes purely from reason, nor is it accumulated by life experiences. The greatest instinct of the mind is called "intuitive awareness" (direct knowing). This is the ability that performs naturally and spontaneously when a person's mind connects with his inner soul. This helps the child to link directly to the experience of wisdom, love, and philosophy he is drawn toward. For instance, a child with musical talent can link with the mind of a great musician of the future who then inspires the child.

In understanding all this, then, we can truly help the children to embrace their inner spiritual power. This is the future of childhood education.

46. PRECOGNITION IS AN INNATE ABILITY JUST LIKE REASONING.

From a rational perspective, the future has not yet come to be and thus it does not exist; but the past is the source of one's experience. With rationalism and logic, we make decisions according to our experiences and the lessons of the past. Via reasoning, we can make proper and wise decisions. This seems to be the only trustworthy way to make decisions for our lives and futures.

However, did you know that rationality is very limited? It must be responsible for all of our decisions but its range is so limited because not only does rationality lack telepathy, but it also lacks precognition. However, it has to make all decisions, such as whether this is a good investment, whether this marriage can be a happy one, and whether to switch jobs. If all of the important decisions in life have to rely on rationality but it knows so little, what can we do when we make a mistake? I suppose this is the reason why everyone nowadays is so worried.

In the book "The Magical Approach," Seth explains thoroughly the essence of time: The past and the future have the same influence as the present. Rationality assumes that the future is both nonexistent and unknowable, and that we can predict the future only by reasoning. But life is ever-changing, and thus the future is not so easily predicted through rationality!

However, within the psyche lies natural human instinct, which means that the future can be sensed. This does not mean that everyone's future is doomed and unchangeable but that the future already exists in a probable way. For example, maybe there are twenty probabilities of how your life will be five year from now, but the "you" of the present can think and take action on only one of those twenty at any given moment to decide which destiny you will have.

Many possibilities lie in the future. Rationality, information, and the accumulation of experiences cannot meet the great challenge of the times any more. Things in the past were simple, and the values and decisions of the time were also simple. In the diverse modern world, however, everyone must make countless decisions amid disturbing and uncertain situations. Thus, the human mind becomes bottlenecked, being more and more confused and uncertain and feeling inadequate to decide anything. Thinking all day long sensibly without any solutions is one of the main reasons modern humans get chronic fatigue syndrome.

From the New Age perspective, the great challenge humanity now faces is to stimulate and evoke future potentialities. A linear conception of time and logical reasoning can no longer solve the problems facing humanity. We will definitely feel much pain if we continue to depend on this old equipment. Thus we must augment our natural equipment—instinct and precognition is as natural as reasoning to the human mind.

Children's minds have the great power of precognition. However, adults often tell children not to speak nonsense. When children mature, they gradually become accustomed to the adult world—oh! Adults do not think that the future is predictable so my ability to predict the future is unnatural, foolish, and unscientific. Therefore, children progressively forget that precognition is equally as correct and natural as reasoning.

If we can understand fully that envisioning a possible future beforehand can help us make the best decision now, we can live our lives better than navigating in the big ocean, losing the direction and with no end in sight.

Interestingly, the future may be forecast but it is not predestined. Each decision you make now relates to which future will come to pass. This butterfly-effect-like world-view that past, present, and future may coexist as probabilities will overcome the obstacles of modern humanity.

Hence, in educating children, assuring them that humans have the ability to predict the future is very important. We should constantly instill correct ideas into children and teach them how to sense accurately the probable futures, so that they may picture their future blueprints in their minds immediately and direct their present focuses toward it. Children will also instinctually understand how their immediate decisions will affect their futures. When human minds can grasp the future naturally, we need not to rely completely on (limited) rationality to make decisions, to often be afraid of the future, or to be scared to make wrong decisions.

47. THE WISDOM OF "WORLD-VIEW".

First, I would like to introduce a word, "world-view," and a very important concept: The reality of spirit is far richer, more useful, and more unimaginable than we have previously assumed.

Now I have to break the following fallacy: Whether in the circles of science, academia, or education, people think that knowledge is acquired by scientific experiments, treatises, academic discussions, reading, or teachers. They think that knowledge and experience are accumulated through time, or learned by sense organs like eyes, ears, nose, tongue and body.

So where are knowledge, experience and wisdom? Since the invention of words and printing, people have come to understand that books are treasures that contain much beauty. Humans started to pass knowledge from one generation to the next via books and schooling. Thus, books have become the medium for people to know what the others are thinking, doing and eating, and to learn from those in ancient times.

If you visit the largest library in the world, which collects books from around the world, you will feel like you are in a treasure-house of human knowledge and wisdom. If you are good at categorizing and searching for information, you may swiftly find the answer to all of your questions and the information you want. However, even if you are diligent in the pursuit of knowledge, you are not likely to finish reading all of the books in ten whole lifetimes.

Now, I'd like to ask you again, exactly from where do knowledge, experience, and wisdom come? You may tell me the results are the records of what people from the past until now have seen, heard, or sought and thought. Today you cannot sit with Lao-Tzu or Jesus to play chess, drink tea, and chat, but you can read Tao Te Ching or the Bible to know what are Lao-Tzu's and Jesus's thoughts on life.

If you are a student of architecture wishing to visit great ancient architects like Lu Ban, Michelangelo, or the living I. M. Pei, but lack money to pay for the travel expenses, you can get inspiration, knowledge, or wisdom only by appreciating and studying their works or by reading their books.

But how about great people in the future? Let's say a distinguished musician will be born two hundred years in the future, and that you are a person with such great musical talent that all of the greatest musicians of the past cannot satisfy your desire to learn: how can you learn from a person who has not yet been born? How can you read masterpieces of music that have not yet been written? How can you hear and feel their fascinating rhythms?

There are very detailed explanations of this in the Seth book "The Nature of the Psyche." Actually, the human ability to learn is not restricted only to the sensory organs. We learn by hearing with ears, seeing with eyes, and touching with skin, but reading words and one person teaching another are only two of the many ways of learning.

Of course, modern people save the contents of books and information on computers. Simply by clicking we can find almost everything on the Internet. However, these ways of obtaining knowledge and information are still based on time and sensory organs. Nevertheless, we still cannot find either the information which has not been put onto the Internet nor the wisdom of the people who have not yet been born.

Returning to the most important concept: Besides material reality, there is a greater, richer, and far more magical spiritual reality. It records all of the knowledge and experiential wisdom about the earth, humanity, culture, art, science, religion, and civilization in a condensed and mysterious way. This treasurehouse of wisdom is the result of the cooperation of every consciousness that has or will live on the earth. From a human's perspective, the life experiences, knowledge, and wisdom of the consciousness which was reborn (regardless of whether or not it has transmigrated), or of those who are going to be reborn (although from our perspective these people haven't been born yet) exist in the form of "world-view" inside the great spiritual reality.

Thus, human potential in this respect has not yet developed. For childhood education, there could be a completely different way to learn: not from external sensory organs but from the development and training of internal sensory organs. Children can surf the Net of spirit, linking their own minds to the great spiritual reality for direct learning. People have not understood this method of learning but, when it appears, the whole of human civilization will have a revolutionary breakthrough and a truly great new era will come.

48. ACTIVATING THE POWER OF THE SPIRITUAL NETWORK.

Let me first talk about the story of the poet Jane Roberts, who transmitted the Seth Material.

Roberts did not have any children in her life because she did not want to have any worries after transmigrating. (This is also the decision that most people in their final incarnation will make, not marrying or not having any child after marriage. However, do not assume that those who do not marry or have no children are in their last incarnation. That would be a big misunderstanding.)

One day before Christmas one year, Roberts was wondering what exquisite gift she should give to her husband, Robert F. Butts. Butts was a professional artist while Roberts painted as a hobby. With her gradually enhanced wisdom and psychic ability, Roberts wanted to know how far her ability might reach. She asked her husband what present he wanted and his reply was "books related to painting."

Therefore, with the love Roberts had for her husband, her own psychic ability, and their common interest in painting, she formed a spiritual energy field. It was a field formed by strong desire and the understanding of the inner psychic reality. Through this "vessel of the psyche," Roberts started to receive Paul Cézanne's world-view from her psychic reality.

Of course, Paul Cézanne is a well-known painter who has already left the physical plane. So the knowledge, skills and insight about the painting of Cézanne, but not the physical person, were what Roberts contacted. And also Cézanne's insights and perspectives made after his death. Thus, we can say that Roberts gained all of the essence of Cézanne's thought and wisdom anent painting, including material from before his life time and after his death.

The information came so fast into Roberts's mind that she could hardly transcribe it. The astonishing content and brilliant viewpoints were totally beyond Roberts's knowledge of painting.

Even professional artists and reviewing artists found it so advanced that they benefited from it.

(People who understand a little about the Seth Materials know that Roberts can be described as the physical body of Seth while she channels Seth. Developmentally, Seth said that he may be considered Roberts's own sixth incarnation in the future, which means that Roberts still has six more stages to pass before she achieves the same state as Seth. For Roberts, this life in which she transmitted the Seth Materials was also her last, physical, incarnation. Colloquially, Roberts was released from physical life and ascended to a higher level of existence.)

Think about it:

Whether or not it has been transcribed, the crystallized wisdom of great people through the ages has become a shared mind and spiritual asset for modern human beings. What a great theory and discovery! If we can teach ourselves and our children to use the power to access this "spiritual network," will this treasure house of wisdom and knowledge not be open to us at any time?

Hence, as an educational ideal in the New Age, learning about the spiritual assets of humans, developing everyone's spiritual ability, teaching each child and adult to embrace a loving heart to help themselves and others with an open, uncritical, and flexible attitude while activating the power of the "spiritual network" should be the most important focus of future education.

In addition, this ability is not constrained by time and space. I hope that people will not think that it is a myth or nonsense or that we are asking you to turn every child into a psychic. In fact, this ability to access the "spiritual network" belongs to all humans. In the past, some people thought of this information source was simply "inspiration" and "enlightenment," some misunderstood it as the words of ghosts or gods. But this is not the truth.

In our children's education, we should let children follow their own nature and allow their psyches to be exposed to as many fields as possible. Further, we should recognize certain types of psychological triggers and use them to stimulate the release of children's inner psychic ability. We should treat them and lead them normally, and help them to receive messages from their inner sensory organs clearly. However, remember: Do not overreact or think of everything received as a precise prediction. Think of it as a correct and healthy development.

* * *

AFTERWORD – EXPLORING WITH CHILDREN
By Dr. Tien Sheng Hsu

In the movie "Love Actually" I saw this scene: A stepfather thought that his eleven-year-old boy was sad and isolated himself because his mother just passed away. He thus asked his son, while sitting on the long bench in the park, whether he wanted to talk about what was in his heart. The little boy answered: "Do you really want to know?" Finally, the little boy said frankly to his father that he was sad not because his mother died, but that it was because he had fallen in love with a girl in his class and he suffered much because of his love. The father became relieved at that point: "I thought it was something big!" Surprisingly, the little boy retorted in a serious manner. "How can love be no big deal? How can suffering because of love not be a big deal?"

The father knew immediately that he had made a mistake, that he was viewing the child's feelings from his own perspective. But what if this father immediately said to his son: "Child, you don't understand that your mother just passed away not long ago! You are giving me trouble already, speaking the nonsense that an eleven-year-old child fell in love and suffered—you had better be good and study hard!" If he said this, we may conclude that from then onward, neither would this child's heart be open nor would he reveal his heart to his father ever again.

Dear parents of today, please think carefully: Exactly how often has a similar situation arisen in your family, and how did you deal with it? Did that lead to a gradual closing of your child's heart to you, and do you still blame your child for not communicating?

At times like this, some fathers might possibly comfort the child and say something that has nothing to do with the issue, such as: "Don't worry, you are young, and there are always opportunities," or make some other casual suggestions.

But here's a father that did nothing like that; instead he acted decisively. First he respected his son's desire to become a rock-and-roll musician in order to win the girl's heart, including his practicing drumming frequently, and accepting the sign his son hung outside of his child's door which read: "I am not hungry, please do not disturb." (I have a question about this: Why are parents always afraid that their children might die of starvation?)

Second, that father decided to explore with his child, to encourage his child not to give up, and to bravely express himself so that, even though he might be rejected, at least he has tried. Furthermore, he took his son into his car, sped to the airport, and asked his son whether he wanted to run through the obstacles at the airport to present himself to the girl for whom he cared.

This is real-life education, one that teaches children to care about what they love, to obtain what they love, and to grow for love. And the process of exploring life with his child seems to have stirred in his father's heart the courage to search for love himself. The father became hopeful to again meet the single mother whom he had met and for whom he had strong feelings.

Actions like this really move me—respecting children's thinking, accepting children's feelings, even using the opportunity to encourage children to grow, without dogma, without preaching, without burdening them with worry or a big fuss.

I encourage all parents and teachers to follow their children's explorations because, with your support and encouragement, your children will not be in any danger, and the exploration itself will open a new dimension in your own lives. It will not only thoroughly dismantle the stale rigid frame of your adult life but also enrich the life you already have, and give you a new perspective, vitality, thoughts, and feelings.

Get a life! Get a life! Allow the children be the guides to open your closed spirits, explore the fresh air of a great spiritual land, follow the children in exploring, accompany the children on their adventure—believe me, you will certainly have some unexpected rewards.

* * *

An Introduction to Seth

The Spiritual Teacher Who Launched the "New Age" Movement

Who is Seth?

Seth is the internationally acclaimed spiritual teacher who spoke through the author Jane Roberts while she was in trance and whose empowering message literally launched the New Age movement. The books written by Seth have sold over seven million copies and have been translated into over a dozen languages. Seth's clear presentation of the furthest reaches of human potential, the eternal validity of the soul, and the concept that we create our own reality according to our beliefs, has rippled out to affect the lives of people in every corner of the globe. Seth's work (first published in the late 1960's) has withstood the test of time and is still considered by many to be one of the most comprehensive, brilliant and undistorted maps of inner reality and human potential available today. If you want answers to life's most important questions, if you want to improve your life conditions, Seth's books will show you how, not by relying on him, but by accessing and using the tremendous source of power and wisdom that lies within each of us.

Reviews from Leaders in the Field
of Human Potential and Consciousness Studies

The Seth books present an alternate map of reality with a new diagram of the psyche... useful to all explorers of consciousness. **Deepak Chopra, MD author of** *Ageless Body, Timeless Mind* & **other bestsellers**

I would like to see the Seth books as required reading for anyone on their spiritual pathway. The amazing in-depth information in the Seth books is as relevant today as it was in the early '70's when Jane Roberts first channeled this material. **Louise Hay, author of** *You can Heal Your Life*

I count Jane Roberts' brilliant book *The Nature of Personal Reality* as a spiritual classic and one of the influential books in my life. As I closed the last page, I looked up at a new world-boundless and filled with possibility. **Dan Millman, author of** *The Way of the Peaceful Warrior*

Re: *The Nature of Personal Reality: A Seth Book*
Quite simply one of the best books I've ever read. **Richard Bach, author of** *Jonathan Livingston Seagull*

Seth was one of my first metaphysical teachers. He remains a constant source of knowledge and inspiration in my life. **Marianne Williamson, author of** *A Return to Love*

"The Nature of Personal Reality: A Seth Book" had an important influence on my life and work. Seth's teachings provided one of the initial inspirations for writing *"Creative Visualization."* **Shakti Gawain, author of** *Creative Visualization*

The Seth Books were of great benefit to me on my spiritual journey and helped me to see another way of looking at the world. **Gerald G Jampolsky, M.D., author of** *Love is Letting Go of Fear*

As you read Seth's words, you will gain more than just new ideas. Seth's energy comes through every page, energy that expands your consciousness and changes your thoughts about the nature of reality.
Sanaya Roman, author of *Living with Joy*

If you are interested in learning about the Seth material, we recommend starting with the three books below or visit our educational websites.

SETH BOOKS
The Seth Material by Jane Roberts
Seth Speaks by Jane Roberts
The Nature of Personal Reality by Jane Roberts

For further information and a complete list of Seth books, online courses, conferences and Seth Audio CD's visit our websites.

www.sethlearningcenter.org – Introduction to Seth, free audio clips of Seth and free CD

www.sethcenter.com – The Seth Bookstore, Seth books and audio CDs & the complete works of Jane Roberts
Phone 516-869-9108

www.sethinstitute.org – Online courses & Conferences
To request our free catalog or for further information contact us at: **Email: sumari@sethcenter.com**
Phone: 516-869-9108

About the Seth Foundation and Seth Clinic in Taiwan
Dr. Hsu runs the Seth Clinic in Taipei, Taiwan, which emphasizes the philosophy and health-care concepts that are inspired by the teachings of Seth. The Seth Education Foundation in Taiwan was founded in March 2008. It offers free talks, provides holistic health-care services to patients, and arranges spiritual growth courses based on the Seth material. For further information see websites:
http://www.drtienshenghsu.com/ (English) or
http://www.seth.org.tw/ (Chinese)

THE SETH AUDIO COLLECTION

THE SETH CLASS SESSIONS (1972-79) are available on CD along with transcripts. These are audio CD's of the actual Seth sessions recorded by Jane's student, Rick Stack, during Jane's classes in Elmira, New York, starting in 1972. Volume I, described below, is a collection of some of the best of Seth's comments gleaned from over 120 of the later Seth Class Sessions. Additional later Seth Class Sessions are available as The Individual Seth Class Session CD's. **For information ask for our free catalogue or visit us online at www.sethcenter.com .**

Volume I of The Seth Audio Collection consists of six (1-hour) CD's plus a 34-page booklet of Seth transcripts. Topics covered in Volume I include:
• Creating your own reality – How to free yourself from limiting beliefs and create the life you want, • Dreams and out-of-body experiences. • Reincarnation and Simultaneous Time.
• Connecting with your inner self. • Spontaneity – Letting yourself go with the flow of your being. • Creating abundance in every area of your life. • Parallel (probable) universes and exploring other dimensions of reality. • Spiritual healing, how to handle emotions, overcoming depression and much more.

Order The Seth Audio Collection at www.sethcenter.com
New Awareness Network, P.O. Box 192, Manhasset, NY 11030.
Or Call (516) 869-9108 9:00-5:00 p.m. Monday-Friday ET

For the complete collection of Seth Books and Audios visit
www.sethcenter.com

Books by Jane Roberts from Amber-Allen Publishing

Seth Speaks: The Eternal Validity of the Soul. This essential guide to conscious living clearly and powerfully articulates the furthest reaches of human potential, and the concept that each of us creates our own reality.

The Nature of Personal Reality: Specific, Practical Techniques for Solving Everyday Problems and Enriching the Life You Know.. In this perennial bestseller, Seth challenges our assumptions about the nature of reality and stresses the individual's capacity for conscious action.

The Individual and the Nature of Mass Events. Seth explores the connection between personal beliefs and world events, how our realities merge and combine "to form mass reactions such as the overthrow of governments, the birth of a new religion, wars, epidemics, earthquakes, and new periods of art, architecture, and technology."

The Magical Approach: Seth Speaks About the Art of Creative Living. Seth reveals the true, magical nature of our deepest levels of being, and explains how to live our lives spontaneously, creatively, and according to our own natural rhythms.

The Oversoul Seven Trilogy (The Education of Oversoul Seven, The Further Education of Oversoul Seven, Oversoul Seven and the Museum of Time). Inspired by Jane's own experiences with the Seth Material, the adventures of Oversoul Seven are an intriguing fantasy, a mind-altering exploration of our inner being, and a vibrant celebration of life.

The Nature of the Psyche. Seth reveals a startling new concept of self, answering questions about the inner reality that exists apart from time, the origins and powers of dreams, human sexuality, and how we choose our physical death.

The "Unknown" Reality, Volumes One and Two. Seth reveals the multidimensional nature of the human soul, the dazzling labyrinths of unseen probabilities involved in any decision, and how probable realities combine to create the waking life we know.

Dreams, "Evolution," and Value Fulfillment, Volumes One and Two. Seth discusses the material world as an ongoing self-creation—the product of a conscious, self-aware and thoroughly animate universe, where virtually every possibility not only exists, but is constantly encouraged to achieve its highest potential.

The Way Toward Health. Woven through the poignant story of Jane Roberts' final days are Seth's teachings about self-healing and the mind's effect upon physical health.

Available in bookstores everywhere.

CPSIA information can be obtained
at www.ICGtesting.com
Printed in the USA
JSHW031524120322
23649JS00005B/164

9 780989 405881